DOG BIZ

Amanda O'Neill

DEDICATION
FOR SUE TAYLOR
AND HOLLY,
WITH THANKS.

The Author

Amanda O'Neill was born in Sussex, England, in 1951 and educated at the University of Exeter, where she studied medieval literature. She has written books on subjects ranging from needlework to mythology, but her abiding interest has always been the world of dogs and cats. She has written more than 20 books on this theme including *The Best Ever Book of Dogs*, *What Dog?*, *Cats and Dogs,* and the companion title to this volume, *Cat Biz*, and she was editor of *The Complete Book of the Dog*. She is a regular contributor to a number of national pet magazines in the U.K.

CONTENTS

DOG BIZ

continued...

SECTION FOUR
Dogs and people 136

LOOKING

AT DOGS

HOW THE DOG BEGAN

In the beginning

Creation myths worldwide link the creation of the dog with that of man, the Creator either having a dog of His own or making Dog specifically to look after Man. An Aboriginal myth says that after the world was formed, it split in two, leaving Man on one side of the chasm and all the other animals on the other. Only Dog was prepared to make the leap across to join Man, and has been his loyal companion ever since.

When were dogs domesticated?

The earliest archeological evidence of dogs is around 14,000 years old. In 1997, geneticists suggested that dogs might have been around much longer than previously believed, inferring from the huge diversity of canine DNA sequences that domestication might have begun as early as 60,000 to 100,000 years ago. However, the latest genetic studies indicate a domestication date of around 15,000 years ago.

Made in China

In 2002, geneticists pinpointed the dog's ancestry to just three female wolves living in or near China nearly 15,000 years ago. A study of gene sequences from dogs' mitochondrial DNA, which is inherited down the maternal bloodline, indicates that 95 percent of today's dogs have a common origin in a single gene pool, traced back to those three wolf bitches—the "Eves" of the dog world.

The "plastic gene"

Dogs come in a wider range of shapes and sizes than any other species, from Chihuahua to Great Dane and from Dachshund to Greyhound. Since we now know that they all started from the same stock, it seems that canine genes are capable of producing and developing mutations faster than that of other animals. Geneticists nicknamed the flexible inheritance responsible for this diversity the "plastic gene."

Who domesticated whom?

One theory is that humans adopted wolf cubs, and over many generations the tame wolves developed into dogs. The other is that wolves adopted humans. Bolder individuals may initially have hung around settlements to scavenge food and then gradually moved in, to live among people as the ownerless pariah dogs of the East do today.

◀◀ *Although Huskies (left) are among the breeds closest to the wolf (far left) and are often described as looking "wolflike," they have a rounder face and shorter jaw—characteristic features of domestication.*

Ancient art

Animals that appear to be curly-tailed dogs rather than wolves are depicted in Neolithic rock art, for example, at Çatal-Hüyük in Turkey, one of the earliest recorded towns with buildings dating back to 6500 B.C. A rock carving at Tassili-n-Ajjer in Algeria clearly shows humans and dogs hunting together, with three dogs and a man with a lance tackling a wild ox.

Buried together

At Ein Mallaha, in northern Israel, archeologists uncovered a 12,000-year-old grave where the skeleton of an old woman lay with its left hand resting on the skeleton of a puppy. We don't know what the relationship was between the two, but this oldest known canine burial suggests that dogs were of some significance to this ancient human.

Kissing cousins

Genetic analysis of dogs and wolves produced surprising results regarding which breeds are most closely related to the ancestral wolf. Of 85 breeds studied, the wolf's closest cousins are the Shiba Inu, Chow Chow, Akita,

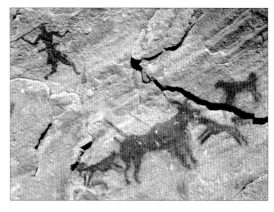

⬆ *Prehistoric rock paintings at Tassili-n-Ajjer depict dogs as the hunter's helper.*

Basenji, Shar-pei, Siberian Husky, Alaskan Malamute, Afghan Hound, Saluki, and Lhasa Apso. Astonishingly, Pekingese proved to be much closer kin to wolves than "wolf-like" German Shepherd Dogs!

⬇ *From left to right: the Akita, Afghan Hound, Saluki, and Chow Chow are among the breeds most closely related to the ancestral wolf.*

THE ANCIENT WORLD

"Breed" beginnings

The oldest known canine image depicting diversity in dog types—the dawn of "breeds"—is a hunting sketch of around 6000 B.C. from the prehistoric city of Çatal-Hüyük in Turkey, which shows long-legged slender dogs evidently built for speed. This "greyhound" type may have been the earliest distinctive variety of dog, though not necessarily the ancestor of our modern Greyhound.

Egyptian diversity

The art of Ancient Egypt depicts an impressive range of canine shapes and sizes. Paintings from 2000 B.C. show heavy "mastiffs," pendent-eared scenthounds, and leggy sighthounds, as well as less differentiated specimens. A few centuries later artists included miniatures and short-legged dogs—the dog had diversified to include novelty "breeds" as well as workers.

◀◀ *Man and dog return from a successful hunt in this 18th Dynasty Egyptian fresco.*

▲ *This Greek bas-relief of c.510 B.C. depicts a familiar scene, as two household pets are introduced to each other—the dog offering to play, the cat more wary.*

Greek heroes

The canine heroes of ancient Greece were war-dogs. Alexander the Great's favorite Molossian hound, Peritas, was said to have killed an elephant and a lion in single combat, and had a city named after him. The city of Corinth, saved from a night attack by its 50 guard dogs, built a memorial to the 49 who died and awarded the lone survivor, Soter, a life pension, a silver collar, and the title of "defender and savior of Corinth."

Blackie and Co

Among the most charming canine relics of Ancient Egypt are the few names of individual dogs that survive in inscriptions. These include (in translation) Blackie, White Antelope, Grabber, Destruction, Reliable, Good Herdsman, Howler, and One Who Is Fashioned as an Arrow. There is even a record of a dog called Useless, who must have had some redeeming virtue to have earned his place in history!

Shrines and sacrifices

The dogs of Greece also gave their lives for religion; they were favorite sacrifices to the gods. Black puppies in particular were offered up to Ares, god of war, and Hecate, queen of the dead. The sacred dogs at the shrine of Aesculapius, god of healing, were luckier: they were honored as divine "doctor dogs" who cured the wounds of sick pilgrims by licking them—and were paid in honey cakes.

...and tiny Roman lapdogs

The Romans appreciated their hounds, herding dogs, and war dogs, but they also loved lapdogs—so much so that Julius Caesar complained of Roman matrons who preferred playing with their lapdogs to bringing up their children. Some historians believe the common warning *Cave canem* ("Beware of the dog") often meant "Don't tread on the lapdog" rather than "Watch out for the guard dog!"

Great Celtic Hounds...

The giant hounds of the Celts were famous— massive dogs that could pull down a stag or a mounted horseman with equal ease. In A.D. 390 a Roman consul who acquired seven Irish dogs reported, "All Rome viewed them with wonder and fancied they must have been brought hither in iron cages." Indeed, a dog's skull found in an Irish bog is said to have been 17 inches (43 cm)—6 inches (15 cm) longer than an average Great Dane's!

⌃ *An enchanting Roman marble depicts two Greyhounds, not as hunters but in a gentler moment, as affectionate companion animals.*

◀◀ *Roman mosaic pavements like this one from Pompeii are not just decorative, but also warn burglars to "Beware of the Dog."*

THE NOSE THAT KNOWS

Super-smell

Smell is the most important of a dog's senses. He has a larger proportion of his brain devoted to scent than we do, and some 220 million scent-detector cells in his nose, compared to our mere 5 million. He can detect scents at concentrations nearly 100 million times lower than we can, recognizing blood diluted at one drop to 5 quarts (4.7 L) of water—although breeds and even individuals vary in their comparative scenting abilities.

⬆ *Scent-marking with urine is the canine equivalent of updating local noticeboards.*

⬆ *Dogs can communicate as much via the sense of smell as we do by chatting to each other.*

Breed variations

Hounds and gundogs are superior sniffers, while short-muzzled breeds and toy dogs are usually less gifted. In one test, researchers released a single mouse in a one-acre field and sent different dog breeds to look for it. Beagles succeeded in one minute, Fox Terriers took nearly 15 minutes, and Scottish Terriers never did sniff out the mouse, although eventually one Scottie found it by treading on it!

Communication by nose

Scent plays an important part in canine communication. Dogs leave scent messages for each other, using urine, feces, and specialized scent glands, from which other dogs can "read" their identity, gender, age, social status, state of health, and even mood. Favored scent-marking points such as trees and lampposts serve as a canine local newspaper, announcing who is in town and what they are doing.

Jacobsen's organ

A dog's sense of smell is backed up by an extra sense. An organ in the roof of the mouth, known as Jacobsen's organ, enables him to "taste" scent particles in the air to obtain more detailed information on particularly interesting smells such as sex pheromones. Although all vertebrates have this organ, it is highly developed in only a few mammals, including dogs, cats, and horses.

Sniffer dogs

In this age of technology, we have yet to invent any detector gadget to beat the dog's nose, and dogs are employed worldwide to sniff out

Finding a needle in a haystack is child's ▶▶ play to the most sensitive canine noses.

particular scents—from drugs and explosives to dry rot, gas leaks, smuggled ivory, foulbrood bacteria in beehives, and even illnesses such as cancer. Scientists have tested species from pigs and coyotes to skunks and ferrets, but none could match canine detectors.

175-year-old scent

In 1987, development work at Fort Erie, Ontario, Canada, uncovered a gravesite where soldiers killed at Snake Hill during the War of 1812 were buried. After archaeologists had located all the graves, Candy, a chocolate Labrador trained as a search dog, was brought in. She immediately located all the known gravesites—plus three more that no one had spotted, sniffing out bodies buried 175 years previously.

Color coding

Dogs' noses can be black, brown ("liver"), pink, or even spotted. Pink ("Dudley") or spotted ("butterfly") noses are frowned upon in many,

▼ *Nose color is linked to coat color, but is also affected by other factors such as temperature.*

though not all, breed standards. Diet and temperature can affect nose pigmentation, causing temporary or permanent fading. Some black noses develop a pink streak in winter, termed a "snow nose," considered undesirable in most show dogs but acceptable in Siberian Huskies.

Sense of taste

The dog's sense of taste is limited, though he can distinguish sour, bitter, salty, and sweet tastes. He has only one-sixth as many taste buds as humans, but three times as many as a cat. This reflects diet: humans are omnivores, cats stick to a strictly meat diet, while dogs fall between the two. The dog's ability to appreciate a sweet taste can be his downfall; most dogs love chocolate, which can actually be fatal to them.

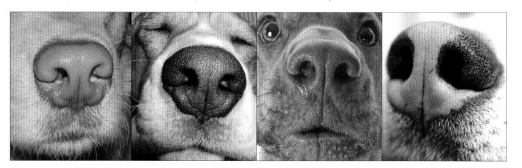

HEAR HEAR!

Superior ears

Dogs have a much better sense of hearing than ours. We register sound frequencies from about 16 to 20,000 Hertz (sound waves per second), but a dog can hear sounds from about 70 to 100,000 Hertz. "Silent" dog whistles are designed to make use of this fact, operating at a range too high for us to hear, but sounding loud and clear to a dog from as far as 500 yards (460 m) away.

Ear shapes

The natural shape for a dog's ear is upright and cup-shaped, designed to direct sound waves toward the middle and inner ear. However, we have bred dogs to have a range of different ear shapes, including erect, hanging, and

⬆ *In some individuals, one ear stands up but the other remains floppy like a puppy's.*

semierect, and ranging from "propeller ears" in Italian Greyhounds, which stick out sideways, to "rose ears" in Whippets, which are folded over and backward.

Ear movements

The natural erect dog's ear is hugely mobile, capable of swivelling toward a sound to pinpoint its direction. Ear carriage is also used to communicate mood, as when ears are flattened in discomfort or fear. The restricted ear movement of dogs with floppy ears, such as spaniels, does not have a major impact on hearing but can lead to communication problems with other dogs.

Ear champion

A Basset Hound named Jack, who lives in Germany, tends to trip over his ears—not surprisingly, as he holds the record for the longest ears in the world, each measuring 13 inches (just over 33.2 cm). Basset Hounds have notably long ears, and previous record holders have been of the same breed, including Biggles, the famous icon of Hush Puppies shoes.

Pendent ears

Ears that hang downward (termed drop, folded, hanging, pendent, or pendulous ears) derive from a genetic mutation that preserves the floppy ears

⬆ *The wide range of ear shapes found in different breeds have been selected because we find them attractive, rather than for practical reasons.*

Long ears, common in scenthounds, were once believed to direct scent towards the nose.

breeds, including Bull Terriers, Dalmatians, Collies, and English Setters. Training deaf dogs poses owners some problems, but reward-based teaching systems using hand signals, body posture, facial expression, and even flashing lights enable many deaf dogs to lead normal and happy lives.

Canine hearing aids

Early experiments with canine hearing aids in the 1980s hit the problem that dogs simply removed the irritating foreign body from their ears and ate it. In 1995, German acoustics expert Hans-Rainer Kurz, developed a model to be implanted in the outer ear, first used by an elderly Beagle named Joschi. It cannot help stone-deaf dogs, but can make a difference for those with severe hearing loss.

of puppyhood. In some breeds this feature has become enormously exaggerated. A belief that hanging ears helped to funnel scent toward the nose encouraged the development of extra-long ears in scenthounds such as the Bloodhound.

Ear cropping

The practice of cropping—cutting off all or part of the outer ear—was introduced in early times to reduce the risk of ear injuries in fights, and later became fashionable. Today this ugly and painful mutilation is banned in many countries, including the U.K. and Australia, but still accepted in others, including parts of the United States, where it is considered to give a "smart" appearance.

Coping with deafness

Sadly, congenital deafness occurs in several

⬆ *Sign language bridges the communication gap for deaf dogs—after all, dogs communicate among themselves largely by body language.*

THE EYES HAVE IT

How dogs see the world

Sight is less important to dogs than it is to us; they "see" the world first and foremost via the sense of smell, and their eyesight differs from ours. We can see details six times better than dogs do, have better binocular vision, and recognize more colors. However, dogs typically have a wider field of vision (apart from flat-faced breeds such as Pekingese) and can see in dimmer light.

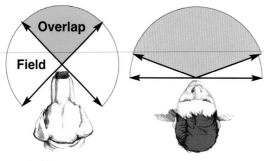

⬆ *Eyes on the side of the head give a wide field of vision, but limited binocular vision (overlap).*

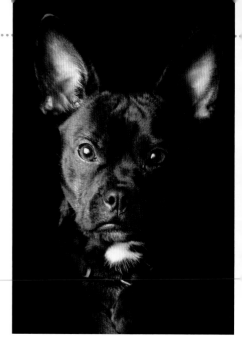

⬆ *The "glow in the dark" quality of dogs' eyes is due to an internal "mirror" reflecting light.*

Color-conscious

Dogs do have color vision, thought to be roughly equivalent to that of a human with red-green color-blindness, but don't use it as much as we do. They can distinguish color at the opposite ends of the visible spectrum (such as red and blue), and even differentiate shades such as blue and violet, but their eyes lack color receptors for green to distinguish between red, orange, and yellowish greens.

Night vision

Dogs have much better night vision than we do. For one thing, their eyes contain more light-sensitive rod cells (and fewer color-sensitive cone cells) than ours. For another, they have a mirror-like layer of light-reflecting cells (the tapetum) at the back of their eyes to amplify what light there is, which is why, when you shine a flashlight on your dog at night, his eyes flash back a brilliant shine.

Third eyelid

Dogs, like cats, have an inner, third eyelid (the nictitating membrane) that slides up over the surface of the eye to protect it and keep it moist. It's normally inconspicuous, held in place by ligaments. Some breeds, such as the Bulldog, tend to a condition called "cherry eye," where weak ligaments let the third eyelid gland slip out of place (appearing as a pink blob in the inside corner of the eye), which needs surgical repair.

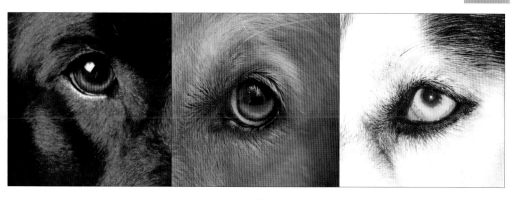

⬆ *Eye color does not affect vision, any more than it does in humans. Breeders select for a particular eye color purely for appearance.*

Eye color

Most dogs have brown eyes, shading from hazel to dark brown. Yellow eyes ("hawk eyes") also occur, while Siberian Huskies are noted for the dramatic blue eyes that some have. Indeed, blue eyes (known as wall, china, fish, jeweled, marbled, or silver eyes) are not uncommon in breeds carrying the merle color gene. Merles may also have flecked or spotted eyes, or one blue eye and one brown.

The crying game

Can dogs cry? They are well equipped to do so, with twice as many tear glands as humans (the extra pair is situated in the third eyelid). Regular tear production is vital to keep eyes moist; malfunctioning glands lead to dry eyes (needing treatment with "artificial tears") or weeping eyes (overproduction). Dogs don't cry from emotion as we do—the large-eyed Pekingese is said to be the only breed that weeps with grief.

What are you pointing at?

Dogs can do something that neither our closest relative, the chimpanzee, nor theirs, the wolf, can manage: they can follow a human gaze or pointing finger to identify a target. When a Hungarian research team compared how dogs and hand-reared wolves located hidden food, it was only the dogs that looked at human faces for clues—a human-type skill picked up over thousands of years of domestication.

Dogs follow the line of ▶▶ their owners' eyes to see what they are looking at, a trait that may have developed through domestication. This terrier takes his cue from his handler to find out what has attracted her attention.

ATHLETIC DOGS

Running dogs

Nature designed the dog as a long-distance runner (the opposite of the cat, which is a sprinter). The basic model dog can travel for miles at a steady, energy-saving trot, breaking into top gear for short bursts only. Of course, humans have developed a range of variations from the basic model, from speed specialists such as Greyhounds to short-legged, underpowered plodders such as Bulldogs.

⬆ *Powerful thigh muscles provide impetus to enable a typical dog to jump his own height.*

⬆ *Dogs love to run, and they need the exercise of free running to develop healthy muscles.*

Racing dogs

Greyhounds are built to make the most of the dog's short bursts of speed. Long legs and a deep chest to accommodate a strong heart and lungs enable them to reach speeds of 45 mph (72 kph). They are not only the fastest breed of dog (twice as fast as a human and nearly as fast as a racehorse) but have better acceleration than any other animals save cheetahs and pronghorn antelopes.

Walking the dog

In an age when many dog owners consider an hour's stroll around the park reasonable exercise, an English Springer Spaniel demonstrated her idea of a decent walk. Four-year-old Cinders accompanied four climbers up and down the five highest peaks in Britain, from Snowdon to Ben Nevis, in the space of 48 hours to raise over $18,000 for cancer research. Never flagging, she led the way and ended her marathon walk in high spirits.

Jumping jacks

Cindy, a Greyhound, holds the record for a high jump at 66 inches (168 cm). In the increasingly popular American sport of dock-diving, when dogs leap off an elevated dock into water, a dog named Country achieved an astounding long jump of 28 feet 10 inches (8.78 m). Dock-diving is open to any breed from Chihuahuas to Newfoundlands, though one Bloodhound entrant simply fell off the dock into the water and walked out.

High climbers...

Some dogs are great climbers. In 1901, U.S. President Theodore Roosevelt was impressed by a pack of hunting dogs that followed lynx and

cougars up trees—particularly Turk, a Bloodhound, who chased a lynx almost 30 feet (10 m) up a pinon tree. More recently, in 1998, Duke, a Border Collie/Australian Shepherd mix from North Dakota entered the Guinness Book of Records for the highest climb (9 feet/2.84 m) up a stack of car tires.

Doggy-paddling

Swimming comes naturally to most dogs,, though some heavily built breeds such as Bassets and French Bulldogs are more prone to sink than float. A few dogs manage to master diving techniques. In 1999, Miss Daisy, a Boxer

The popular agility ▸▸ challenge of weaving between poles demands a highly supple spine.

from Derby, England, hit the headlines for her diving skills after she taught herself to stay underwater for more than 30 seconds, diving to the bottom of a pool to retrieve toys.

Skipping and weaving

Dogs can also manage some nifty footwork. Olive Oyl, a Borzoi from Illinois, has learned to skip over a rope, and in 1998, she managed a record 63 consecutive skips in one minute. Another fast mover is Jazz, a Border Collie from South Africa, who holds the record for the fastest time weaving between 60 poles, which he managed in 12.98 seconds in 1999.

Marathon swim

In 2002 a two-year-old black Labrador named Todd was presumed drowned after he fell overboard from his master's boat near the Isle of Wight off the English coast. Six hours later he paddled wearily ashore only 10 miles (16 km) from home, having swum the same distance to the mainland and then upriver in an amazing feat of navigation, ignoring much nearer landfalls in order to head directly homeward.

▼ *Not many dogs swim underwater. Hamish, a West Highland White from Hampshire, U.K., is the world's first scuba-diving canine.*

THE TALE OF THE TAIL

A variety of tails

The ancestral wolf has a long, bushy tail carried low when at rest; the pariah-type dog, which is thought to resemble the earliest domestic dog, has a tail curled high over its back. Beyond these basic types, man has developed dogs with an astonishing wide range of tails—long, short, or absent, straight, twisted, or curly, thickly plumed or bare as a rat's.

What use is a tail?

Tailless or short-tailed dogs don't seem to be physically disadvantaged, but where a tail is present it is a useful extra. It serves as a balancing aid when the dog is running, enabling him to swing around a corner without losing momentum, and it also serves as a rudder when he is swimming. More importantly, it is a means of communication: tail language expresses emotions loud and clear.

⬆ *The tail serves as a counterbalance in a range of activities, although dogs without tails seem to compensate very well.*

Odd tails

Breed standards stipulate a range of tails from corkscrew to pothook. Among the most unusual is the hairless tail that earns the

Telling Tails	
Tail position	**Meaning**
Horizontal but not rigid	Interest
Horizontal and rigid	Cautious greeting, prepared to challenge or be challenged
High but not rigid	Confidence
High and rigid	Assertive
High, rigid, and bristling	Aggression
Below horizontal but not touching legs	Relaxation ("neutral gear")
Down, near hind legs	Worry or depression
Tucked between hind legs	Fear
Wagging—broad, sweeping movement	Friendliness

Wagged out

Most sporting dogs display enthusiastic tail action while working, but a good day's hunting can leave some dogs completely "wagged out." In particular, Labradors, Pointers, Setters, Foxhounds, and Beagles are prone to "frozen tail" (also termed "limber tail" or "coldwater tail"), a condition in which overused tail muscles give up, leaving the tail hanging limp. Fortunately, most recover after a few days' rest.

Docking

Humans have docked dogs' tails for centuries, for various reasons, including superstition (cutting off the tail was thought to prevent rabies), practicality (to prevent tail injuries in working dogs and soiling in long-coated breeds), and mere fashion. Today, docking is banned in many countries and the subject of controversy in others. Traditionally, docked breeds are beginning to become familiar in tailed versions.

⬆ *The tail is also a highly expressive means of communication—and, of course, a great temptation to mischievous puppies, as this patient older dog has discovered.*

otherwise curly-coated Irish Water Spaniel his nickname of "Rat-tail." Other oddities include the tightly kinked short "screw tail" found in Bulldogs and Boston Terriers and the uniquely flattened tail of the Chihuahua.

Tail language

Dogs communicate a great deal by the position and movement of their tails, but allowances need to be made for breed differences. Some breeds, such as Huskies, naturally carry their tails high; others, such as Collies, are bred for a low tail carriage. We also need to appreciate subtleties of expression. We think of a wagging tail as the equivalent of a human smile; but we should remember that not all smiles mean the same thing.

⬆ *Boxers have been traditionally docked since the breed was first developed, and many Boxer breeders still prefer a docked tail.*

A FUR FUR BETTER THING

Two coats or one

Most dogs are double-coated, with a thermal vest of soft hairs next to the skin and a topcoat of long, weather-resistant guard hairs, averaging a total of 1,000 to 6,000 hairs per square inch (2.5 cm). Extra undercoat produces softer fur, extra guard hairs create a rougher texture, while single-coated dogs, lacking undercoat, feel silky, whether long-haired (Maltese) or short-haired (Italian Greyhound).

Excess coat

One of the hairiest breeds is the Old English Sheepdog, whose shaggy coat needs three or four hours' grooming a week—and much more if he is to appear in the show ring. In the old

days, farmers used to tackle the coat by shearing their dogs along with the sheep. Today, many Old English are passed on to rescue societies when owners find the coat more than they can handle.

Dogs with perms

Curly coats are generally associated with water dogs, providing extra waterproofing. Curly-coated retrievers have easy-care "wash and dry" curls, while Irish Water Spaniels have dense ringlets that need careful grooming. Long-coated curly breeds like the Spanish and Portuguese Water Dogs are often clipped for ease of care and to prevent waterlogging—and, of course, for fashion.

Dogs with dreadlocks

The long dense curls of the Komondor mat into dangling cords, forming a completely weather-proof coat similar to that of the sheep this powerful livestock guard herded in his native

⤒ *The Old English Sheepdog's glamorous coat evolved as a practical weatherproof jacket for a tough farm dog working in harsh conditions.*

◀◀ Antonio the Bergamasco displays his coat of dense, flat, ribbonlike "flocks," which take four to five years to achieve their full, floor-length glory.

Hungary. It is a high-maintenance coat—mats form naturally, but must be separated out by hand to form the characteristic cords. It takes two years to form a correctly corded coat, which eventually flows right down to the ground.

Armor-plated dogs

The coat of the Bergamasco Sheepdog, an Italian herding breed, is also matted, but rather than cords it forms broad, flat sections which eventually reach the ground, providing both weather-proofing and effective armor-plating against wolf attacks. Washing a Bergamasco in readiness for a show is a marathon task: the coat can take a couple of days to dry!

Canine Rapunzel

Poodle clips are often exaggeratedly stylized, and may look ridiculous to non-Poodle owners, but there is a reason

▲ The Lion Clip is based on a working trim, with longer fur protecting chest and joints.

behind the clip. Unclipped Poodles end up buried under a mound of hair, because their hair just keeps growing. At one time, owners would clip their initials into the coat! Left to itself, the hair forms cords like a Puli's. Corded Poodles used to appear in the show ring, and are occasionally exhibited today.

Recycled dog hair

When grooming a long-haired dog, it's easy to fill a bag with combings. This hair can be spun (at home, or professionally) into a high-quality yarn up to 80 percent warmer than sheep's wool. Combings need to be at least 2 inches (5 cm) long, preferably undercoat, and are often mixed with sheep's fleece to make a soft, light wool—nicknamed "chiengora" from French *chien* ("dog") and Angora.

The Chinese ▶▶ Crested has hair only on head, tail, and paws, and his bare skin needs the same beauty care as ours.

Bald facts

Hairless mutations have occurred several times across the world, giving rise to a few breeds, of which the best-known are the Mexican Hairless and Chinese Crested. Although hairless dogs feel the cold, they can be tougher than they look: Adam, a champion Chinese Crested, lost for a week in the middle of a Swedish winter, survived in the snow, at temperatures of −13°F (−25°C), in remarkably good shape.

A GOOD DOG IS NEVER A BAD COLOR

Canine color palette

Dogs come in black, black-and-tan, brown, red, golden, gray, white and patched, spotted, or dappled variations of these colors. Breed standards often stipulate exact shades, from the "dead grass" of the Chesapeake Bay

Retriever to the "roe gray" acceptable in the Weimaraner. However, the terminology can be confusing: the same shade of brown may be "liver" in one breed, '"chocolate" in another.

◀◀ *In Labrador Retrievers, brown coloration is always termed "chocolate"—an increasingly popular color in this breed.*

Color prejudice

In Boxers, white dogs have been banned from the show ring since 1925, though many early Boxers, and some 20 percent of Boxer puppies today, are white. Originally, whites were

considered unsuitable for police work; today breeders point to the fact that many white Boxers are deaf. In German Shepherd dogs white is also a disqualifying color, although some countries now accept the White German Shepherd as a separate breed.

◀◀ *White German Shepherds are frowned on by show breeders but have a long history.*

Great Danes are never spotted, but ▶▶ *can be white with black patches, a color termed Harlequin.*

Colorless dogs

Although white dogs abound, albino dogs are relatively rare. Whether a dog is classed as white or albino depends on the skin—most white-furred dogs have dark skin, whereas albino dogs have no pigmentation at all, giving pale skin, nose, and eye rims and blue or pink eyes. White is frowned upon in some breeds, such as the Boxer, but has been selectively bred for in others, such as the Samoyed and West Highland White Terrier.

Spotted dogs

"Spot" is a traditional dog name, but spotted dogs are unusual; most are patched or blotched with color. The Dalmatian is actually the only spotted breed. Not all Dalmatians have the evenly sized and spaced spots associated with the breed; some are mismarked, and may even have large patches of color, which disqualify them from a show career but don't stop them from making great pets.

Blushing breed

Fancy a dog that turns pink? The Pharaoh Hound is the obvious candidate, being famous as the only dog that blushes. When happy or excited, these bat-eared sighthounds really do blush, their ears turning bright rosy pink and the flush developing down their faces to turn their naturally pink noses a deeper shade.

Pharaoh Hounds are ▶▶
always a rich tan or
chestnut, with white
markings allowed.

Rhapsody in blue

Blue (actually subtle shades of light to slate grey) typifies Kerry Blue Terriers, and also occurs in breeds such as Great Danes. Attempts to breed a blue Pekingese foundered on the standard's insistence on black noses (never found in blues), though one pre-war specimen, Alderbourne Rhapsody in Blue, was hailed as "priceless" and sold for the then record price for a three-months-old puppy of over $1,800.

⩔ *Shetland Sheepdogs are among*
the breeds that display the
beautiful blue merle coloring.

Marbled merles

The merle gene found in some breeds produces a marbling effect on coat color, with irregular dark blotches against a lighter background. The best-known shade is the blue merle, with black patches or streaks on a blue-gray ground, but red merles, cream merles, etc., are also found. Merles can be very beautiful, but are not favored by all breeders because breeding merle to merle can produce blind puppies.

Louisana leopards

Louisiana's state dog, the Catahoula Leopard Dog, is one of the most unusually colored breeds. Both "Leopard" patterns and blotched "Patchwork" patterns are caused by the merle gene, which also accounts for the favored "glass" (blue) eyes. Formerly known as the Catahoula Cur, the breed takes its name from the striking blue-eyed spotted variety, although it also comes in solid colors and brindles,

ONLY NATURAL

Social life

Wolves are social animals that naturally live in family groups and socialize with friends, relations, and casual acquaintances just as we do, which is why their descendant the dog fits in so well with human lifestyles. The canine social structure was once thought to be a rigid ranking system from top dog to underdog, but it is now considered to be more of a "family" structure with a great deal more to it than just dominance and submission.

⬆ *Herding is really hunting behavior that stops short of capturing and killing the "prey."*

⬆ *Socializing matters to dogs, who benefit from mixing with their own kind as well as with us. All dogs should be socialized from puppyhood.*

"Peter Pan" wolves

Domestication changes animals. Later generations are often more juvenile in their appearance and behavior than their wild ancestors, perhaps because of selective breeding focused on the friendliest, most co-operative or most easily handled specimens. Consequently, domestic dogs act, and often look, more like juvenile wolves than like adult wolves.

Hunters and herders

Specialist working dogs from gundogs to Collies derive their skills from their wolf ancestors' co-operative hunting instincts. The pointer's stylish frozen stance when he marks game is an overdevelopment of the wolf's momentary freeze on spotting prey, while the Border Collie's intense herding drive, crouching posture, and hypnotic "eye" all arise from the way wolves work together to drive herds of game.

Walkies

Wolves are travelers. The territories where they roam may be vast—in wild places such as Alaska the average pack territory covers 600 square miles (1,550 sq km) and a day's journey may cover 20 miles (32 km) or more. It's hardly surprising that their domestic descendants still need physical exercise and the mental stimulus of exploration. Don't just take your dog for an on-leash stroll around the block—give him a real walk

Playtime

Scientists have a lot of theories about why animals play, from using up excess energy to practicing vital skills. Wolves are playful creatures, and one reason may be that play reinforces social bonds, just as when dogs play with their owners. The dog's playful nature is a valuable tool in training sessions, if lessons are presented as games: the "Fetch" exercise can be just as much fun for the dog as simply chasing a ball.

Guarding

Wolves guard food, den sites, packmates, and cubs, and dogs have inherited the same instinct, though various breeds display a stronger or weaker guard drive. Dogs have been renowned over the ages for defending their masters, though people have often abused the dog's protective side, imagining that treating a dog kindly will reduce its guard instinct, or expecting a full-fledged guard drive in a baby puppy.

Retrievers

Why do retrievers bring game back to their masters, and pet dogs relish playing "Fetch"? Again, this is based on natural behavior. Wolves

▼ *Playing "Fetch" is a natural behavior, and also a marvelous opportunity for exercise.*

carry food back to the den for cubs and adult "baby-sitters" that have remained at home. Meat is usually carried in the stomach, and served up by regurgitation, but a whole rabbit or a deer's leg is brought by mouth—and wolves also carry back non-food items as toys for their cubs.

Playtime and schooltime ▶▶ *should be combined.*

Caring and sharing

Wolves are devoted and patient parents, and most well-adjusted dogs extend this caring instinct to their human families. Assistance dogs trained to help the physically handicapped astound watchers by the way in which they actively look out for new ways to help. Even untrained pets may do the same, like Holly, a West Highland White who, seeing her owner falling into a diabetic coma, fetched jelly beans to raise her blood sugar levels.

COMMUNICATION

Body language

The body language of posture and movement makes up a large part of canine communication. Broadly speaking, confident, dominant, or aggressive dogs make themselves look as big as possible; timid or submissive dogs make themselves look small, and may also use puppy signals such as offering a gentle muzzle-nudge to demonstrate how harmless they are.

⬆ *Puppies have to learn how to communicate with other dogs just as children learn to talk, but they never acquire a full wolf vocabulary.*

Puppy talk

Dogs communicate so well with us that it's surprising to realize what a small vocabulary they have. Their vocal range is limited to just ten different sounds (only a tenth as many as cats) and their whole lexicon of voice, gesture, and expression is smaller than that of the ancestral wolf. In fact, dogs use the "baby talk" of wolf cubs, not the full range of expression used by adult wolves.

⬆ *Instantly recognizable body language, the "play bow" is a friendly invitation to a game.*

Doggy dialects

The latest report from scientists suggests that dogs pick up local accents from their owners. For example, a study of the barks of hundreds of British dogs showed a regional variation in pitch and tone correlating to their owners' voices, with Scotland and Liverpool supplying the most distinctive canine accents.

◀◀ *Researchers believe dogs pick up their owners' accents as part of the bonding process.*

Tail talk

A dog's tail is wonderfully expressive, but we can sometimes misunderstand what it says. Many people believe that a wagging tail means happiness and friendliness, but certain types of wag signify fear, worry, or aggression. We also need to allow for breed variation; for example, most gundogs wag more enthusiastically than herding breeds, while docked or tightly curled tails have limited expression.

Secret language of smells

We can translate a great deal of our dogs' vocal and body language, but our noses aren't up to reading the language of smells, which is also a key part of intercanine communication. To a dog, sniffing a scent-marked tree or lamppost is equivalent to reading a local newspaper packed with messages and gossip about their neighbors' status, age, gender, social life, associates, recent activities, and even mood!

Telling tales

A Japanese legend says that in the beginning dogs talked just like humans, but one day Dog told his master that his mistress was having an affair, and the angry wife punished him by taking away his human speech. Since then, dogs have been able only to bark—although some gifted individuals have learned to mimic a few human words, such as "Hello," "Mom," or "Sausages."

The little dog laughed

It came as no surprise to most dog owners when scientists announced, in 2005, their discovery that dogs do actually laugh. "Play panting" by happy dogs is now recognized as canine laughter. Experiments at a dog shelter in Washington State showed that playing recordings of "laughing dogs" to stressed inmates reassured them within minutes and helped them to relax.

Translating machine

Japanese inventors have created the Bowlingual, a canine translation device to convert barks and whines into human speech via a microphone and voice print analyzer, with programs adapted to different breeds. Complete with a guide to body language, medical checklist, and tips on dog training, it quickly became a best-seller.

⬆ *The Bowlingual has different settings to interpret the barks of various breeds.*

PUPPIES

Multiplication problems

Dogs are dependent on us to prevent too many puppies from being born. A bitch may come into season as early as six months of age, producing puppies while she is only a baby herself, and thereafter can have two litters a year until she is well into old age. On average, an unspayed bitch could have 64 puppies in her lifetime, wearing herself out and of course adding to the problems of dog shelters.

How many?

Litter size depends on breed. Two puppies may be a good number for a toy breed; bigger breeds may have a dozen or more. A Neapolitan Mastiff named Tia achieved a record in 2004 with her litter of 24, of which 20 survived (*below*). Of course, males are far more prolific. Between December 1961 and his death in November 1969, a racing Greyhound called Low Pressure sired 2,404 registered pups—plus at least 600 unregistered ones.

Paternity puzzles

A bitch can mate with, and conceive by, more than one male when she is in season, meaning that puppies born in the same litter may have different fathers. This may go unnoticed in crossbred litters, but a surprise package in a pedigree litter may call for DNA testing to ascertain exact parentage before the puppies can be registered.

Color schemes

Puppies are rarely born the color they will end up. Blonde puppies may darken, black puppies

AGE		PUPPY DEVELOPMENT *This is a guide only—breeds vary!*
0–2 weeks	Neonatal period	Totally dependent on mother. Senses of touch and taste present from birth.
2–4 weeks	Transitional period	Eyes and ears open. Starts to stand, toddle, bark, growl and wag tail. Eyesight well developed by 4th or 5th week.
3–12 weeks	Socialization period	Interaction and play with littermates. Physical co-ordination improves; dawn of social skills. Weaning around 6 weeks. Needs exposure to people, noises, household activities.
3–6 months	Ranking period	Development of status and rank order. Teething period (and chewing!) with second teeth.
6–18 months	Adolescence	Exploring social rank and challenging for position; beginnings of sexual maturity.

Foster mothers

Bitches with puppies are often so full of mother love that they are ready to adopt orphans of other species, including what would normally be prey animals ranging from birds to rabbits. Huahua, a Chihuahua from Guizhou province, China, adopted a baby chick, while a number of zoos have called in canine foster mothers to raise exotic infants from lion and tiger cubs to meerkats.

⬆ *Born white, these baby Dalmatians are just beginning to develop their spotting.*

become lighter, markings appear or disappear, and in some breeds black puppies may even end up white. Dalmatians are born white, developing their spots from about ten days old, whereas Soft-coated Wheaten Terriers are born black, and may take two years to complete the change to wheaten.

Party time

Puppies that miss out on social experience never catch up, and are likely to have behavior problems later. To help owners with socialization, many dog clubs now offer "puppy parties" where puppies can mingle like playschool children. These can be invaluable, but check that they are well run before enrolling; without proper supervision, your puppy may learn only that play is more fun than listening to you.

⬆ *An unusual fosterling! Meg adopted a baby owl, and looked after her like a puppy.*

BREED FACT FILE

When breeds began

Although there were distinct types of dog way back in ancient times, breeds were not formally defined until the 19th century. Until that time, a dog's ancestry mattered less than whether he could do his job, from gundog to lapdog, and breeders did not hesitate to cross different types to achieve that end. It was only when Britain's Kennel Club was founded in 1873 that breed standards and registration of pedigrees were set up.

⬆ *The terrier puppy and small collie type shown in* Introductions *by Charles Henry Tenre don't conform to any modern breed standard.*

The lost breeds

Many breeds once well known disappeared without ever achieving Kennel Club recognition, local strains such as the Norfolk Spaniel, unglamorous workers such as the Smithfield Collie, and disreputable types such as Glasgow's fighting dog, the Blue Paul. Others were transformed or absorbed into breeds we know today, the English Black and Tan Terrier into the Welsh Terrier, the Clydesdale into the Skye.

How many breeds?

Worldwide, there are some 400 breeds of dog, but most countries have to be satisfied with about half of that number. The American Kennel Club recognizes 208 breeds (including 51 "rare breeds" awaiting full recognition), and the British Kennel Club, 201 breeds.

Breed groups

Kennel Clubs categorize breeds into groups by function. The U.S. and U.K. both recognize seven groups, not always with the same names: Gundogs/Sporting, Hounds, Working (guards, draft dogs, etc.), Terriers, Herding, Toys, and Non-sporting (breeds that don't fit into any of those classes). However, some breeds are ascribed to different groups in different countries.

UNDERSTANDING BREED TERMINOLOGY	
Breed	A race of dogs with similar genetic makeup, sharing fixed characteristics and reproducing these consistently.
Pure-bred	A dog all of whose ancestors belonged to the same breed.
Crossbred	A first- or second-generation cross between two different recognized breeds.
Mongrel	A dog of mixed ancestry and no identifiable breed.
Pedigree	Record of ancestry. We speak of "pedigree dogs," meaning dogs belonging to a particular breed, but not all purebreds have pedigree papers, while some crossbreds and even mongrels may have, if breeding records were kept.

Geographers' despair!

Accurate geography is rarely a factor in naming dog breeds. The Great Dane is a German breed, not Danish, and the Australian Shepherd *(below)* is American. The French Bulldog evolved in Britain (although it was not appreciated until it was introduced to France), and the Dalmatian has no connection with Dalmatia; indeed, the breed was unknown there until 1930, when Dalmatians were imported from the U.K.

Creating new breeds

New breeds arise for a variety of reasons. In 1950s Germany, the desire to recreate the basic, unexaggerated Spitz led to the development of the Eurasier from a mix of Samoyeds, Chow Chows, and Wolf Spitz. Around the same time in California, the Kyi-Leo began as an accidental mating between a Lhasa Apso and a Maltese, the resulting puppies inspiring their breeder to develop a new breed from them, which is yet to be formally recognized.

A breed in the making

For those who admire wolves, but recognize that wolves (and most wolf-dog hybrids) are unsuited to pet life, British breeders set out in the 1980s to produce a wolf look-alike by crossing German Shepherd Dogs, Siberian Huskies, and Alaskan Malamutes. There are now some 5,000 of these handsome dogs, known as Utonagans, in Britain and the United States, but the breed has some way to go before achieving official recognition. Some breeders favor a different type of wolf-dog, the Tamaskan.

SIZES, SHAPES, AND STATISTICS

Heavyweights...

The Mastiff is the most massive of the giant breeds. Hercules, a Mastiff from Massachusetts, officially the biggest dog alive today, weighs 282 pounds (128 kg) and has a neck the size of a man's waist, at 38 inches (96.5 cm). An English contender, Zell, is slightly smaller but also slightly heavier at 286 pounds (130 kg). Neither matches up to a previous record-holding Mastiff from London, England, Zorba, who reached 319 pounds (145 kg)!

◄◄ *Zorba the giant Mastiff still remains the heaviest dog on record.*

Only his bearskin ►► *gives this soldier the advantage in height over an Irish Wolfhound.*

...and other giants

The Irish Wolfhound is generally considered the world's tallest breed of dog, with a shoulder height for males of at least 32 inches (81 cm) and often more. However, the tallest individual dog alive today is a harlequin Great Dane, Gibson, from California, 42.2 inches (107 cm) high at the shoulder—and 7 feet, 2 inches (218 cm) when he stands up on his hind legs.

Miniatures

The world's smallest dog breed is the Chihuahua, 6–9 inches (15–23 cm) tall and weighing 2 pounds (0.9-2.7 kg). However, another mini breed, the Yorkshire Terrier, with a similar height and a typical weight of 3 pounds (1.4–3.2 kg), sometimes produces even tinier individuals. The smallest dog on record was a 1940s Yorkie the size of a matchbox, standing 2.5 inches (6 cm) high and weighing just 4 ounces (113 g).

Unusual records

Buddy, a Cocker Spaniel from Michigan, holds the record for the world's longest eyelashes—a stunning 4.7 inches (12 cm) long, beating the previous record-holder by 1 inch (2.5 cm). Another Michigan canine, a Boxer named Brandy, hit the news in 2004 for boasting the longest tongue on record, at 17 inches (43 cm). As she demonstrated on TV, this enabled her to eat from a dish 13 inches (33 cm) away— though it made her a messy eater!

DOG BIZ

...and other extremes

The most unpronounceable breed must surely be the Polski Owczarek Nizinny (usually shortened to PON or translated as Polish Lowland Sheepdog). The most accident-prone, according to a recent report from a pet insurance company, is the Rottweiler, and the least accident-prone the Poodle in all its three sizes.

Ugliest dog

Sam, an elderly Chinese Crested Dog, became an international celebrity after winning a California contest for the "ugliest dog" three years running. Blind, buck-toothed, wrinkled, and warty, Sam had been pronounced unadoptable by a rescue shelter before Susie Lockheed became his proud owner and discovered that ugliness is only skin deep.

Today's tinies

There are two contenders for the title of Smallest Living Dog. Whitney, a Yorkshire Terrier

◄◄ When the Chihuahua was discovered in Mexico in the 19th century, its tiny size led to claims that the breed was a canine-rodent hybrid.

from Essex, England, wins in terms of height, measuring only 3 inches (7.6 cm) at the shoulder, while Danka, a Long-haired Chihuahua from Slovakia, wins in terms of length, being only 7.4 inches (18.8 cm) long. Both were born to normal-sized parents and have normal-sized littermates.

Extreme appendages

Dachshunds have the shortest legs of any breed—and they're getting shorter. Modern show Dachsies are much shorter in the legs than their ancestors, or their working contemporaries—in some exaggerated cases, so much so that their underparts scrape on the ground as they walk. In contrast, the longest legs belong to Great Danes, Greyhounds, and their kin.

SCENTHOUNDS

Ancient lineage

Long before Classical times, breeding and working a pack of hounds had developed from the mere pursuit of food into an art form, with huntsmen seeking not just efficient hunters but stylish ones. Special types of hound for different jobs evolved early; by c.1200 B.C. an Egyptian scribe was able to describe a pack made up of two distinct types, while Greek and Roman writers provide us with 65 different "breed" names.

Kings' favorites

Medieval kings and nobles loved the hunt and kept enormous packs of hounds, which were highly prized. Most famous of all was Souillart, belonging to Louis XI of France (1423–1483), acclaimed as the ideal hound. When old age saw an end to his hunting days, Souillart enjoyed a luxurious retirement with the Grand Seneschal of Normandy, sleeping in his master's chamber and even having a poem written about his feats in the field.

Hound music

Shakespeare wrote of hounds "matched in mouth like bells," and for centuries huntsmen have valued tuneful voices. In the 17th century Gervase Markham recommended a "choir" of large hounds with "deep solemn" bass voices, smaller hounds with "roaring, and loud ringing" counter-tenors, and "hollow plain sweet" medium voices, plus "a couple or two small singing Beagles, which as small trebles may warble amongst them."

Running dogs

Foxhounds are born to run—during the hunting season in Britain, a pack may run 40 to 60 miles

⬆ *Foxhounds are bred for both the speed and the stamina to accompany mounted hunters.*

(65-100 km) on each hunt, usually twice a week. Since they are bred to work with mounted hunters, they have speed as well as stamina. In 1862, the famous Foxhound Blue Cap is said to have covered 4 miles (6.5 km) of Newmarket Racecourse in just over eight minutes—about the speed of a Derby winner at Epsom.

⬆ *Basset Hounds bred for the show ring have even shorter legs than those used for hunting*

The low-set hound

Basset Hounds aren't designed for speed. Their short legs, the result of a form of dwarfism,

France has produced more breeds of hound than any other country, including the Bloodhound (far left) and Basset Artésien Normand (left).

for tracking men. In the 19th century, two Bloodhounds were brought to London to track Jack the Ripper, but were not allowed to make the attempt; perhaps the Ripper's identity would no longer be a mystery if they had been! Today, several police forces employ Bloodhounds as trackers.

No otters for Otterhounds

The Otterhound, said to date back to the 12th century, is a hardy dog bred for water work and capable of swimming for up to five hours in pursuit of his quarry. In 1978, the breed lost its employment when otter hunting was banned in Britain. In need of a career change, some Otterhounds turned to the show scene, while others continue hunting, but now for the purpose of controlling escaped mink.

slow them down enough to allow huntsmen to follow them on foot. They originated in France, and still bear a French name (*bas set* meaning "low-set")—but the modern Basset Hound is an English variety. The original French breed, the Basset Artésien Normand, is smaller, lighter-boned, and much less doleful-looking.

Pocket hounds

Smallest of the scenthounds, the Beagle is a highly popular pet and perhaps the best adapted of all hounds to household life. In the 16th century, even smaller Beagles were fashionable. Rabbits were hunted by packs of "pocket" Beagles, small enough to be carried to the field in a huntsman's pocket—or for a whole pack of ten or twelve couples to ride in his saddle baskets!

Trackers

Bloodhounds developed as scent specialists to find game for the running hounds, but by the 13th century, their superb noses were also used

19th-century Otterhounds at work, portrayed by Sir Edwin Landseer (1802–1873). Today the breed no longer hunts its original quarry.

RUNNING DOGS

In the Middle Ages, hunting was an aristocratic pursuit and the Greyhound an aristocrat itself, "sweet, clean, joyous, willing, and gracious."

Noble history

Sighthounds—long-legged, deep-chested dogs built for speed—developed early in the canine calendar, perhaps around 5000–4000 B.C. in Mesopotamia. For thousands of years they were the hounds of the nobility. In the East; the Bedouins' Saluki was exempt from the classification of dogs as "unclean" in the West, King Canute's Forest Laws of 1016 forbade any but noblemen to own Greyhounds.

The Great Celtic Hound

The giant war dogs of the Celts were famous in the ancient world. They were exported to Rome to fight in the arena, and tradition says that when St Patrick sailed from Ireland to France in the 5th century, he was in charge of a cargo of these hounds. They are claimed to be ancestors of both the Irish Wolfhound and the Deerhound, but at some distance; both breeds had to be "reconstructed" in the 19th century after almost dying out.

Speed merchants

Greyhounds are not only the fastest dog breed but, with a top speed of around 45 mph (73 kph), faster than any other animals but cheetahs and pronghorn antelopes. They have incredible acceleration, hitting top gear in three strides, and astonishing cornering ability. A Greyhound at full gallop is truly flying; it is airborne, with all four feet off the ground, for three-quarters of each stride!

Track racing of Greyhounds began at Tucson, Arizona, in 1909.

Swift as a bird...

In 2001, a race was arranged between Althea Storm, a racing Greyhound, and Speckled Jim, a champion racing pigeon specially trained to fly straight along a racetrack. The Greyhound won, taking 5.3 seconds to complete the 260-feet

(80-m) course at Wimbledon Stadium, with the pigeon on his heels finishing less than a second behind.

Imperial favorite

In Czarist Russia, Borzois were owned only by the nobility, who devoted whole estates to breeding, training, and hunting sighthounds swift enough to catch hares and tough enough to tackle wolves. Hunting was on a grand scale, with magnificent kennels housing hundreds of Borzois. When the serfs who tended the dogs

⬆ *The Borzoi takes its name appropriately from a Russian word meaning "swift."*

were set free in 1861, and again during the 1917 Russian Revolution, most of these aristocratic kennels were destroyed.

What big ears you have...

The Mediterranean regions have produced various local sighthound strains with erect ears, such as the strikingly colored Ibizan Hound. These bat-eared greyhounds look so much like the dogs portrayed in Ancient Egyptian art that they were thought to be direct descendants and one breed, from Malta, was even christened the Pharaoh Hound, but genetic studies have since shown them to be modern creations.

A very fast dog suitable for ▶▶
hunting on all types of terrain,
the Ibizan Hound is the
rabbiting hound of Ibiza and
the Spanish mainland.

"The poor man's Greyhound"

The Whippet, a smaller cousin of the Greyhound, developed at the opposite end of the social spectrum as the poor man's pot-filling dog, catching rabbits to feed his family. In the 1700s, Whippet racing became popular among miners in the north of England. The dogs were taught from puppyhood to play with rags, which served as the lure for races; hence their nickname of "rag dogs."

The poacher's dog

The Lurcher was the British poacher's secret weapon, a sighthound crossed with a sheepdog, terrier, or other working breed to create the ultimate all-round hunting dog, fast and clever. In the 19th century, owning such a dog practically branded a man as a poacher, but today Lurchers are appreciated as wonderful companions. Favored crosses range from Greyhound-Collies to Bedlington-Whippets.

GUNDOGS

Falconers' dogs

The gundog's task is to find game for hunters, not catch it himself. Gundogs developed long before guns, working with falconers, not shooters, and the modern falconry revival has seen a return to this role. Today, Britain alone has some 2,000 falconry dogs, mainly spaniel and pointer breeds. Dog and falcon or hawk work as a team, with the dog finding and flushing out game for the bird.

⬆ *Sir Edwin Landseer's* Serving the Guns *depicts a Pointer and Gordon Setter after the hunt.*

⬆ *Medieval falconers employed the ancestors of our spaniels, setters, and pointers to find and flush out game for their hawks.*

Specialists...

British gundog breeds evolved into specialists. Setters and pointers freeze in stylized poses to mark game, retrievers have "soft mouths" to carry game undamaged, and smaller, brisker

A retriever practices his working skills, ▶▶ *fetching a training dummy from a lake.*

spaniels rummage through undergrowth. Today spaniels' keen noses and enthusiasm for work are employed to detect drugs, bombs, etc., while retrievers' intelligence and trainability make them ideal service dogs for the blind and the disabled.

...and all-rounders

On the Continent, specialized gundogs were less in demand than all-rounders, classed as HPR ("Hunt-Point-Retrieve") breeds and now popular worldwide. These include the Hungarian Vizsla, Weimaraner, Brittany, and German Shorthaired

and Wirehaired Pointers. Two Italian HPR breeds of rather houndlike appearance, the Bracco Italiano and Italian Spinone, are said to be considerably older.

Water dogs

A number of breeds have been developed to retrieve in water as wildfowlers' and fishermen's dogs, from Irish and American Water Spaniels to Spanish and Portuguese Water Dogs *(above)* —and including the Poodle, rarely worked today. One that has moved out of the gundog group is the Newfoundland, whose aquatic talents are now often directed toward life-saving, rescuing swimmers in difficulties.

Golden legend

Legend has it that Golden Retrievers are descended from Russian circus dogs purchased by the first Lord Tweedmouth in the 19th century. History, however, records that Lord Tweedmouth developed his strain of yellow retrievers from a yellow Wavy-coated Retriever called Nous and the now-extinct Tweed Water Spaniel. Today, this handsome gundog is one of the most popular companion breeds.

A dog for all seasons

More than any other breed, the Labrador Retriever has found employment everywhere, as sniffer dog, guide dog for the blind, assistance dog for the disabled, and, above all, companion. He is a dog of many virtues, but there is a downside: Recent research conducted by a pet insurance company concluded that chocolate Labradors are the most accident-prone breed in the United Kingdom!

⬆ *Newfoundlands are often trained for water rescue, retrieving swimmers in difficulties or towing boats and life rafts to shore.*

Cocker confusion

Everyone knows the Cocker Spaniel. But in the 1800s, defining a Cocker was harder. The first Kennel Club stud book classified them by weight alone: spaniels weighing under 25 pounds (11.3 kg) were classed as Cockers, heavier specimens as Field Spaniels. Even when Cockers became a distinct breed, American and English varieties were so different that in 1946, the American Cocker had to be given separate recognition.

TERRIERS

Made in Britain

Although the Bulldog is the national British emblem, a terrier would be more appropriate. Britain had its small, scruffy working terriers long before the Bulldog—certainly by Roman times. All the world's terrier breeds originate from British stock, even modern creations such as the Australian, Japanese, Brazilian, and American Toy Terriers.

⬆ British regional terrier breeds include the fold-eared Norfolk and prick-eared Norwich, formerly considered a single breed.

Bite the Romans!

In the third century, Roman author Oppian recorded that the British kept small "Agassaean" dogs to pursue quarry underground. They were very ugly, he said, with sharp claws and venomous teeth. Canine historians disagree whether these were early terriers, or just unpleasant dogs. Of course, Oppian may have been biased; it is easy to imagine a British terrier getting in a quick nip at the heels of the Roman invaders.

Dark dungeons and close caves

Terriers (Latin *terra*, "earth") are "earth dogs," underground workers. Their task, as defined in the 16th century by Dr. Johannes Caius, is to "creepe into the ground and… make affrayde, nyppe and byte the Foxe and the Badger in such sorte, that eyther they teare them in peeces with theyre teeth being in the bosoms of the earth, or else hayle and pull them perforce out of theyre ducking angles, dark dongons and close caves…"

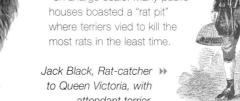

The rat pits

In the early 19th century, ratting was a popular sport on a large scale. Many public houses boasted a "rat pit" where terriers vied to kill the most rats in the least time.

Jack Black, Rat-catcher ▶▶
to Queen Victoria, with
attendant terrier.

⬆ Public ratting contests endured into the 20th century, the last occurring in 1912.

Top ratters became famous, like Tiny, who wore a lady's bracelet for a collar but killed 200 rats in record time, and the famous Billy, slayer of 100 rats in 5.5 minutes, who was invited to Buckingham Palace to be presented to the Prince Regent's daughter.

Playing the Jack

Everyone knows Jack Russell Terriers *(above)*—or do they? The name, originally signifying a type of working Fox Terrier, was misapplied for many years to any small, mainly white mongrel terrier. Kennel Club recognition in the 1990s brought confusion, with different types (long-legged and short-legged) selected by different countries and the breed name varying through Parson Jack Russells, Parson Russells, and Jack Russells.

The Scottish clan

Scotties, Cairns, and West Highland Whites are all offshoots of the same clan of rough-haired Highland Terriers. Today, they are quite distinct, the Cairn being closest to their mutual ancestor in appearance. Early Scotties were much more like black Cairns than the long-coated, large-

▲ *Distinct breeds today, West Highland Whites, Scotties, and Cairns share the same ancestry.*

headed modern breed, while the Westie was a local color strain said to have been favored after a red dog was shot in mistake for a fox.

Hound in disguise?

When is a terrier not a terrier? Some would say when it's an Airedale, Although this handsome dog is nicknamed "King of the Terriers," he is far too big for traditional terrier work—and when did you ever hear of any other terrier undertaking police and military service, or hunting grizzlies in the States? Some experts believe he originated as a wire-haired Otterhound, later made to resemble a giant terrier.

DRAFT WORKERS

Pulling power

As anyone who has tried to walk an untrained dog on leash knows, dogs have great pulling power—indeed, the canine weight-pulling record is over 10,000 pounds (4,500 kg). Humans have harnessed this strength for centuries. In the frozen North, dog sleds were until recently the only means of transport; in milder climates, dogs have pulled anything from milk carts to children's carriages.

⬆ *Roald Amundsen's 1910–1911 expedition to the South Pole was only made possible by the use of dogs to haul the gear and provisions.*

A hard life

Until recently, polar explorers depended on dogs. In June 1910, Norwegian explorers embarked from Oslo with 100 Greenland sled dogs to trek to the South Pole. Dog handler Helmer Hansen commented afterward, "For us humans driving to the South Pole was just like play, but it was no fun for the dogs." It was an understatement. Only 18 dogs survived to reach the Pole in December.

Alaskan heroes

When the town of Nome, Alaska, was hit by diphtheria in 1925, sled dogs were its only hope. Lifesaving serum from Anchorage, more than 1,000 miles (1,600 km) away, was rushed part-way by train, but only dogs could cover the last 674 miles (1,085 km). In appalling conditions, 22 relay teams of dog sleds raced against time and arrived in six days, halving the previous record. Balto, leader of the final team, is still remembered as a national hero.

Great races

The first recorded sled dog race was held in Nome, Alaska, in 1906. Today, races are held from Switzerland to Scotland. Best known is the 1,150-mile (1,850 km) Iditarod from

⬇ *Huskies love to run but can rarely be trusted off leash, so sled racing gives them the opportunity to really enjoy themselves.*

Anchorage to Nome, established in 1973 to commemorate the Nome Serum Run, a marathon that calls for dogs to run up to 125 miles (200 km) a day, usually in six-hour stints, for nine to 14 days, pulling a heavy sled in demanding Arctic conditions.

Dog carts were a common means of transport in the 18th–19th centuries and are still in use in some parts of Europe.

Transport workers

In 18th- and 19th-century Europe, dogs were widely used to pull tradesmen's carts. In wealthier circles, children rode in little carts like goat carts, pulled by one or two strong dogs, while a few eccentric British sportsmen boasted carriages pulled by dog teams. Newfoundlands, Leonbergers, Rottweilers, and Swiss Mountain Dogs were all popular draft breeds.

British ban

The use of dogs as draft animals on public roads was banned in England in 1840, partly on humanitarian grounds—overworked dogs were often driven until they collapsed, then abandoned—and partly to relieve traffic congestion. The ban was not altogether to the dogs' advantage—a partial ban in central London in 1839 led to the destruction of more than 3,000 working dogs.

A healthy hobby

Today, many people enjoy training their dogs for draft work as a hobby. Bernese Mountain Dogs pull their traditionally decorated milk carts, Siberian Huskies race with lightweight wheeled rigs where no snow is available, and a range of other breeds are entering the field. Even toy breeds can have a go with miniature carts; Chips, a tiny orange ball of fluff, boasts the title of Germany's First Carting Pomeranian!

The Bernese Mountain Dog is the most popular carting breed, able to pull its own weight with ease. Owners can demonstrate their dogs' prowess in Draft and Carting Tests.

HERDING DOGS

A long history

A Norwegian legend says that long ago two dogs, watching people trying without much success to gather up a herd of reindeer, decided, "We could do that better," and volunteered their services. Historically, this is pretty much what happened. The pack-hunting technique of driving herds to pick out a selected "victim" comes naturally to dogs, a trait that early man must have found invaluable, as do farmers today.

▲ *The drover and his dog were already an old-fashioned scene when Heywood Hardy (1843–1933) painted* The Handsome Drover.

▲ *Top to bottom: Lapponian Reindeer Herder, Swedish Lapphund, Icelandic Sheepdog.*

relied on their dogs to direct huge herds of cattle or sheep across the country and to guard their earnings after delivery. Often these sagacious dogs made their own way home afterward, taking perhaps a week to travel from London to Scotland and stopping at inns en route for their meals.

How the West was won

Fans of Western films are familiar with the 19th-century "Sheep War," when the arrival of thousands of sheep changed the face of the Wild West. With the sheep came sheepdogs—British collies, and Basque sheepdogs, emigrants from Spain to Australia and then to the U.S. These dogs found a vital role on U.S. ranches, and their descendants became the all-American breed confusingly named the Australian Shepherd Dog.

Drovers' dogs

From the Middle Ages to the 20th century, beef to feed British towns was transported on the hoof, often for hundreds of miles. The drovers

Rustler's assistant

New Zealand's most famous outlaw was sheep rustler James Mackenzie; but it was his dog Friday that did his work, stealing the sheep unaided at night while he established an alibi in a local pub. When Mackenzie was caught with 750 stolen sheep in 1855, he escaped, and angry locals wanted to hang Friday in his stead. She was reprieved, perhaps because no one else could employ her for rustling; she only obeyed commands in Gaelic.

◄◄ 19th-century sheepdogs who made farming New Zealand's hill country possible are honored by a statue at Lake Tekapo.

vast hilly paddocks of New Zealand sheep stations. They drive livestock by barking— they can bark all day—and also use a "backing" technique, running across the backs of a close-packed mob of sheep to direct them.

Fairy steed

The Welsh Corgi is best known today as a royal pet, but it was once a cattle herder, known as the *Ci-llathed* ("yard-long dog"—a Welsh yard of 40 inches/102 cm being its length from nose to tail) or *Ci sawdlo* ("heeler"—a dog that drives cattle by nipping their heels). More romantically, legend says that in ancient times it was the fairies' steed—and the marks of a "fairy saddle" are still carried by many Corgis.

Collie fashions

There were once many local strains of collie, most now extinct, including the shaggy Welsh Grey, the drovers' Smithfield, the handsome red Welsh Hillman, and the Highland Collie beloved of Queen Victoria. Today, the name "collie" is reserved for three very different breeds: the workaholic Border Collie, the show dog Rough Collie, and the Bearded, which has both show and working strains.

Sheepdog trials

Great Britain's first sheepdog trials were held in 1873 at Bala, North Wales, and despite the "most cold, wet and unfavourable" day, drew entrants from "the far north" of England—and 300 spectators. The winner was Tweed, a black and tan Collie who also won the class for handsomest dog. Second was Chap, a dog so small that he arrived in his owner's coat pocket and had to be held up to see the sheep!

Barking and backing

Different breeds of sheep and different terrain require sheepdogs with different working styles. New Zealand Huntaways evolved to work in the

▲ Herding sheep over large expanses of land would be impossible without the help of dogs.

GUARD AND PROTECTION DOGS

Development

With its canine nature to protect home and family, dogs have been valued as guards since ancient times. Big, powerful guard dogs have been selectively bred for courage, loyalty, and a strong territorial instinct, along with aggressiveness and an innate suspicion of strangers. Today, we value good temperament rather than ferocity, and modern guard breeds can be great companions.

◀◀ Rarely chosen as a working guard today, the Bullmastiff is still highly protective of his family.

size more than ferocity to deter intruders. The breed almost died out in the 18th century, to be revived with an admixture of Alpine Mastiff (St. Bernard) and Bulldog blood as a bulkier, less athletic but very imposing giant.

The mighty Mastiff

Mastiffs might be considered the ultimate canine guards, with a long and checkered history as war dogs and fighting dogs, but the modern Mastiff is a gentle giant that relies on

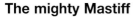

▲ The ancestors of the Mastiff (above left) were the original protection dogs, but the Rottweiler, (above right) is more suited for the role today.

German Shepherd Dogs

The favorite guard breed of the 20th century, the German Shepherd Dog was a general farm worker until it was "discovered" by dog breeders at the end of the 19th century. The distinctive modern show type is very different from its ancestors, and has been joined by unregistered longcoats, whites (given separate recognition in some countries), and the Shiloh Shepherd, an American attempt to breed back to the old type.

Only bad owners

Rottweilers suffered a bad press after the breed became fashionable with would-be macho owners, but in the right hands their protective instincts make them loyal companions. Rotties are not just guards. They excel at a range of tasks from herding to therapy; Gunner, a search and rescue Rottie, received the AKC Hero Dog Award in 2001 for his work at the World Trade Center disaster in New York.

Protection, not aggression

It's a common mistake to imagine that a good guard dog has to be fierce. An aggressive

Flock guardians

A special group of guard dogs is made up of livestock guards such as the Pyrenean Mountain Dog, Maremma, Sheepdog, and Anatolian Shepherd Dog. Developed in countries where flocks and herds need to be defended from predators, they are not herders, but dedicated guardians that live with their flocks. Since the 1970s the use of traditional flock guardians to safeguard livestock has become increasingly widespread.

Guarding cheetahs

Livestock guards can also help to protect predators. Put simply, if wolves can't attack flocks successfully, shepherds are less motivated to kill wolves. In Namibia, Anatolian Shepherd Dogs are working to save endangered cheetahs by guarding goats and sheep from attack. Local farmers who used to shoot cheetahs on sight now spare them, knowing that their flocks are safe.

⤊ *A burglary victim in Syracuse now relies on a ferocious guard dog to defend his home.*

animal is a liability, not a protector, whereas a well-brought-up family pet may be the best defender of the home. Another error is to expect a puppy to do an adult's job—puppies are meant to be friendly. In any event, an alert toy breed is often just as good a burglar deterrent as any guard dog.

⤊ *The Cheetah Conservation Fund supplies Namibian farmers with Anatolian Shepherd puppies to raise with their flocks as guards.*

SPITZ BREEDS

Dogs of the North

Spitzes evolved in the arctic regions as workers —hunters, herders, and sled dogs—and form a distinctive family that includes some of the oldest breeds. Although they come in a range of sizes, from burly Malamutes to dainty Poms, they are all handsome, sturdily built dogs with foxy or wolflike heads, thick fur, and bushy tails, usually curled, and strong, independent personalities.

know it as a Chinese breed, but old Chinese manuscripts describe it as "the foreign dog." Geneticists have now established that this unique dog is one of the oldest breeds, closest to the ancestral wolf.

Honey, I shrunk the dog

As recently as Victorian times, Pomeranians were quite big dogs. English breeders became fascinated by the occasional smaller specimens

🔺 *Among the biggest Spitz breeds is the Alaskan Malamute (left), powerful "carthorse of the North," some 30 times the size of the smallest spitz, the Pomeranian (above right).*

Dog or bear?

The Chow Chow is so unusual, with its bearlike build, blue tongue, unique dentition (44 teeth instead of 42) and odd stilted gait, that it was once thought to be descended from bears rather than dogs. Its history is also obscure: we

that cropped up from time to time, and bred from these to create, in a remarkably short time, one of the smallest toy breeds. Once a working farm dog, the amazing shrinking Pomeranian is now an enchanting ball of fluff weighing as little as 4–5 pounds (1.8–2.3 kg).

Canine contortionist

The Norwegian Lundehund developed in the Lofoten Islands as a specialized hunter of puffins—a staple of the islanders' diet. To catch

↥ *The unique Lundehund had nearly died out by World War II, and remains a very rare breed.*

puffins in their clifftop tunnels demanded incredibly supple dogs. The Lundehund was selectively bred for flexible neck joints allowing it to twist its neck back along the spine, forelegs that rotate sideways, and extra toes with three joints (like our fingers), making it a champion contortionist.

Designer Spitz

The Eurasier is a modern creation, a medium-sized dog developed in the 1960s by German breeder Julius Wipfel, who crossed Chow Chows and Wolfspitz, adding a dash of Samoyed, to produce an unexaggerated companion Spitz breed. Formally recognized in Europe in 1973, this attractive dog has now been introduced to the U.S. and the U.K. and looks set to become better known.

Confused nationalities

How do you tell a Japanese Spitz *(right)* from an American Eskimo Dog? The answer is, with great difficulty. Both are national types of German Spitz, imported to Japan in the 1920s and to the U.S. in the 19th century. In fact, the Eskimo was still known as the German Spitz until World War I, when it acquired a new name on political grounds (just as, in the U.K., the German Shepherd dog was hastily renamed the Alsatian).

Bear hunter—and helper

The Karelian Bear Dog is a Finnish strain of Russian Laika, a large hunting dog with a reputation for tackling big game, especially bear. In the U.S., its talents have been put to a new use, to protect bears. Karelians are trained in "bear shepherding" techniques to train wild bears to recognize and avoid human territory, preventing the tragedy of half-tame bears being shot as dangerous to humans.

Hunting Spitz ▶▶ *include bear and elk specialists, the Karelian Bear Dog (top) from Finland, and Swedish Jämthund (below).*

BULL BREEDS

Bullbaiting

The practice of setting dogs to attack a bull was a popular "sport" from at least the 14th century—sometimes even a legal requirement before a bull was slaughtered, as it was held to make the meat more tender—and it was not banned in the U.K. until 1835. The tough, athletic dogs bred for the purpose gave rise to a range of breeds including fighting dogs, hunters, guards, and even lapdogs.

⬆ *No longer either ferocious or athletic, the Bulldog is now a good-natured companion.*

⬆ *Bulldogs were bred and trained to seize the bull by the nose and hang on. They were often killed or seriously wounded in the attempt.*

Terrier tragedy

The Staffordshire Bull Terrier *(right)* is among the most popular breeds today for contrasting reasons: He is a great family dog (nicknamed "the nanny dog" for his gentleness with children) but also macho enough to appeal to would-be toughs. Sadly, he has become a victim of his own success. More Staffies are bought and then abandoned by unsuitable owners than rescue schemes can accommodate or rehome.

Controversial Bulldogs

The modern Bulldog has a unique personality, but undeniable physical disabilities. While show breeders defend the characteristic short-faced, wrinkled, bowlegged variety, others have attempted to breed back to "the original Bulldog." Modern variations such as Regency, Victorian, and Old English Bulldogs are reconstructions, not recognized by Kennel Clubs but growing in popularity.

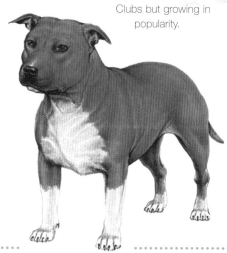

Bouncing Boxers

We rarely think of the Boxer as a bulldog, but the breed was developed from heavy German Bullenbeissers ("bull-biters") and English Bulldogs. Originally viewed as a guard, the Boxer proved his worth as an army dog in World War I. Despite his gladiatorial origins, he has the good nature of so many bull breeds and is now best known as an excellent, if energetic, family dog.

Ban the bull

Powerful dogs in the wrong hands can be dangerous, and governments have begun to tackle the problem by legislation—not against criminal owners but against dogs, and bull breeds in particular. An incident in 2000, when a German drug dealer's dogs killed a six-year-old, led Germany to outlaw four bull terrier breeds. Thousands of innocent dogs were put down; the criminal owner received a mere 42-month sentence.

Night dogs

The blend of Bulldog and Mastiff produced the powerful guard breed we know as the Bullmastiff. Tradition says this breed evolved as the "Gamekeeper's Night Dog" that accompanied keepers on their nightly patrols to watch out for and apprehend poachers, often armed and desperate men. In the 1920s, they were valued as police dogs, although today, most Bullmastiffs work simply as home guards.

Fashionable Frenchies

British dog breeders made a big mistake in the

◄◄ *The bat-eared French Bulldog is a gentle, low-energy breed.*

19th century when they rejected undersized bulldogs as runts and mongrels. When emigrant Nottingham lacemakers took their "toy" bulldogs with them to France, the comical little dogs quickly became fashionable in that country. Thereafter, French breeders who worked to standardize the breed took the credit for what became known as the French Bulldog.

American Gentleman

In America, another offshoot of the bat-eared mini-bulldog strain became the smart little Boston

Terrier *(above)*—who bears no resemblance to the terrier family, despite his name. Originally the Boston Bull Terrier, he changed his name after protests from Bull Terrier fanciers who wanted no connection with this dapper little dog. He is better suited by his nickname: "the American Gentleman."

TOY BREEDS

Ancient lineage

Miniature dogs, of no practical use whatsoever and kept purely for pleasure, have been with us since at least Ancient Egyptian times. They have been valued as living hot water bottles to warm the bed and relieve stomachaches, and as decorative accessories, but their main function has always been simply to give and receive love. Indeed their old title of "comforters" is more appropriate than that of "toys."

Real men don't own lapdogs...

For much of history, mini-dogs have been viewed as ladies' accessories. Julius Caesar accused Roman matrons of preferring lapdogs to babies, while Elizabethan physician Dr. Johannes Caius dismissed toy breeds as mere "instruments of folly... to satisfie the delicatenesse of daintie dames." Men preferred to be seen with big dogs—sporting or guard breeds.

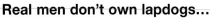
▲ Italian Greyhounds may look frail, but they are no couch potatoes and enjoy an active life as much as their big cousins.

◄◄ The Duchess of Alba, painted by Francisco Goya in 1795 with her attendant lapdog, a Löwchen wearing a matching red ribbon.

Oh yes, they do

Men have never been immune to the charm of smaller dogs. Breeds like the Miniature Pinscher, Brussels Griffon, and English Toy Terrier evolved from men's ratting companions, while tough Yorkshire millhands developed the Yorkshire Terrier, vying to produce ever tinier and longer-coated pets. As the saying goes: Any wimp can own a pit bull—it takes a real man to walk a Chihuahua.

Immortalized in verse

Perhaps the earliest lapdog known to us by name was Issa, a little white "Maltese" dog owned and adored by Publius, Roman Governor of Malta in the first century A.D. No less a poet than the great Martial preserved her memory in an ode that proclaims, 'Issa is purer than a dove's kiss... gentler than a maiden... more precious than Indian gems."

An Irish legend

Cormac's Glossary, a 10th-century Irish manuscript, tells how lapdogs came to Ireland. British law forbade giving such dogs to the Irish, but canny Irish hero Cairbré Musc smeared his dagger haft with grease, lured a lapdog into chewing it, and claimed the dog in recompense for the damage. He bore his prize back to Ireland, calling it Mug-Eimé, "the slave of the haft," where it was much admired and the Irish kings vied for its puppies.

Lapdogs at court

By the Renaissance, lapdogs were the companions of kings. Henri III of France carried a basketful of Papillon puppies hung around his neck, and Pugs were the favorite breed of the Dutch Royal House of Orange. Frederick the Great of Prussia adored his Italian Greyhounds, while Charles II of England so loved his toy spaniels that a long-suffering courtier snarled, "God bless Your Majesty—but God damn your dogs!"

Toys that work

Toy dogs aren't just ornaments. Their small size and general alertness make them ideal

Toy breeds make ideal Hearing Ear dogs who can perform tasks like answering the telephone.

Hearing Ear dogs, while some have proven successful service dogs for the disabled, assisting wheelchair-bound owners with tasks such as answering the telephone, opening and closing doors, even unloading washing machines. In fact, in 1999 the U.S. National Service Dog of the Year was a tiny Papillon named Peekaboo.

⬆ *The red and white Blenheim Cavalier King Charles Spaniel always has a white forehead lozenge—the Duchess' legendary thumbprint.*

Thumbprints

Legend says Blenheim King Charles Spaniels acquired the white lozenge on their foreheads in 1704, when the Duke of Marlborough fought the Battle of Blenheim. His Duchess, clutching a spaniel for comfort, left her thumbprint on his forehead, a mark passed on to future generations. Similarly, in Pekingese, a white spot on the foreheads is said to be the mark of Buddha's thumbprint.

ORIENTAL BREEDS

Ancient heritage

East is East and West is West, and their dogs are distinctly different. Broadly speaking, the Oriental breeds tend to be more independent-minded and less obedience-oriented. Many of them seem to regard themselves as our equals rather than our pets, which may be explained by geneticists' discovery that Eastern breeds are often more closely akin to the ancestral wolf than most Western breeds.

Pekingese

Most exotic of toy breeds, the Pekingese was for centuries the companion of Chinese emperors, often with a higher status than most human courtiers. In the 2nd century A.D., Emperor Ling Ti gave the rank of viceroy to his palace dogs and awarded his favorite Peke the official hat of the highest literary grade of the time— a hat almost as big as the dog!

"Buddha's thumbprint" on the forehead and a startled expression typify the Japanese Chin.

◀◀ Two of the great emblems of Imperial China: the Pekingese and the chrysanthemum.

century, when they were discovered by the Western world, these little dogs with "butterfly heads, sacred vulture feathered feet, and chrysanthemum tails" were kept by the nobility alone. They were kept in hanging birdcages as living ornaments, or carried in baskets lined with blue silk.

The Dog Shogun

In 17th-century Japan, Shogun Tokugawa Tsunayoshi was nicknamed "the Dog Shogun" for his devotion to dogs. Deeply concerned with animal welfare, he made cruelty to animals a criminal offense. His animal protection laws extended down to mosquitoes but, having been born in the Year of the Dog, he made dogs his special concern and set up kennels to home more than 50,000 stray dogs at public expense.

Japanese Chin

Japanese Chins clearly share a common ancestor with Pekingese, but have developed along much daintier lines. Until the mid-19th

Tibetan trio

The breeds we now know as the Tibetan Spaniel, Tibetan Terrier, and Lhasa Apso were treasured in the monasteries of Tibet. They

Shih Tzu ⬇

◀◀ *Lhasa Apso (far left) and a Tibetan Spaniel (left).*

were useful as lookouts and bodywarmers, but were also valued as bringers of good luck. It is said that they were never sold, but only given as valued gifts. The Dalai Lama took his Tibetan Terrier, Senge, with him when he was forced to leave Tibet.

Exotic mixture

What has the head of a lion, the face of an owl, the eyes of a dragon, the mouth of a frog, the torso of a bear, and the back of a tiger? The answer is the Shih Tzu, according to an early Chinese "breed standard." Canine historians disagree whether this hairy little dog originated in China or Tibet. Certainly he is a close relative of Tibet's Lhasa Apso, indeed, the two breeds were considered one when they first reached the West.

Sumo wrestlers

The Japanese Tosa was bred for dogfighting, not the bloodthirsty sport of the West, but dog wrestling, in a similar style to Sumo wrestling. This is an ancient tradition, once used to inspire

Samurai warriors. The Tosa himself is a later creation of the 19th century, a cross between native and Western breeds. Matches are very formal, with the dogs arriving in ceremonial robes, and fighters are disqualified for barking or growling.

Considered a ▶▶ *National Treasure in his native Japan, the Tosa is banned in many countries.*

DOG SHOWS

The beginning

The origins of dog shows can be traced to informal competitions at local fairs as early as the 16th century, or to hound shows, first recorded in the late 18th century, but shows as we know them began in early 19th-century London taverns where, as a spinoff from popular dogfighting and ratting contests, dog-lovers held meetings to judge breeds of "Fancy Pets" on looks alone.

Tykes in taverns

An early tavern "dog show" was held at the Elephant and Castle, London, in 1834, when "9-pound (4 kg) spaniels" competed for a silver cream pitcher. A show at "a public house in Denmark Street" in 1851 made it into the *Illustrated London News,* whose reporter scorned the dogs on show—King Charles Spaniels ("for sporting purposes… good for nothing"), Italian Greyhounds ("quite useless"), and Skye Terriers ("shapeless little monsters").

⬆ *A large entry at the 1963 Championship Show of the Ladies Kennel Association in London.*

National shows

The first British show to draw a truly national entry was the First Exhibition of Sporting and Other Dogs at Birmingham, West Midlands, in 1860, which attracted 267 dogs and 7,800 spectators. Three years later, the public flocked to Islington, London, to see "The First Great International Dog Show"—a six-day event attracting 1,678 entries. The dog show had arrived!

Gundogs to Newcastle

In 1859 the annual poultry show at Newcastle-upon-Tyne in northeast England introduced a dog section with two classes, for Setters and Pointers. Sometimes claimed to be the first "real" dog show, its actual significance lay in the fact that, for the first time, competitors arrived from all over the country, thanks to the introduction of the railroad. However, both classes were won by local dogs.

Ladies first

In male-dominated 19th-century Britain, the foundation of the Ladies' Kennel Association in 1894 was seen by many as "absurd in conception and inept in practice." Despite this attitude, titled ladies and royalty supported the LKA and indeed dogloving Queen Victoria became Patron. The U.K. Kennel Club, founded in 1873, was for men only, and remained resolutely so until as recently as 1979.

Charles Cruft—and, right, the Crufts 2005 Best In Show winner, Norfolk Terrier Ch. Cracknor Cause Célèbre, sitting in the Best In Show cup.

Crufts

The world's biggest and best-known dog show is Crufts, in London, brainchild of dog biscuit salesman Charles Cruft. It started in 1886 as a Terrier Show, but when it was opened to all breeds in 1891, it drew 2,437 entries, including a number from Queen Victoria's own kennel. The famous Best In Show award was not introduced until 1928, when it was won by Primley Sceptre, a fawn Greyhound.

Westminster

The Westminster Dog Show, held in New York, is America's equivalent to Crufts. Although inspired by the success of dog shows in England, it predates Crufts, having begun in 1877, after the Kentucky Derby, the oldest continuous sporting event in the United States. Westminster even beat Crufts to the introduction of a Best in Show award, first presented in 1907 to Ch.Warren Remedy, a Smooth Fox Terrier.

Australia

Australia's first dog show took place in Hobart, Tasmania in 1862. This Canine Exhibition attracted 91 dogs of at least 17 breeds, including an "Esquimaux Poodle." The next recorded dog show, and first on the mainland, was run by the Acclimatisation Society "to encourage Improvement in the Breed of Dogs" and to discourage the keeping of "useless curs." Held in Melbourne in 1864, it attracted 381 dogs.

◄◄ *A lineup of Shih Tzus await judging at the 129th Westminster Dog Show, 2005, watched by a huge crowd of spectators.*

PARIAHS AND PRIMITIVES

Pariah dogs

The ownerless dogs living as "urban wild animals" around human settlements in Asia and Africa are known as pariahs or pi dogs. Breeding without human intervention, they show a fair amount of variation and certainly don't comprise a breed. However, the classic medium-sized, curly-tailed, ginger pariah is a recognizable and ancient type, probably very much like the earliest domestic dogs.

Canaan Dog

In the 1930s, some of Israel's pariah dogs found themselves part of a domestication project designed to produce the ideal military dog for local conditions. A true-breeding strain was established that satisfied the army's requirements for guards, trackers, and mine detectors, and, under the name of Canaan Dog, later achieved KC recognition to prove equally successful in the show ring.

⬆ *India's pariah dogs live alongside humans, scavenging a living from garbage, much as their ancestors did thousands of years ago.*

⬆ *Israel's feral dogs, descendants of herding and guard dogs of Biblical times, were redomesticated to produce the Canaan Dog.*

Naturalist's dog

When Indian naturalist Billy Arjan Singh adopted a pariah dog, he acquired not only an inseparable companion but an assistant in his conservation work. Eelie helped him to raise big cats and other animals in his home and prepare them for release into the wild. Hunting and playing with leopards, wolves, and even a tiger, the little pariah dog was able to bridge the gap between the world of man and that of the wild.

Singing Dog...

The Dingo-like native dog of New Guinea in the 1950s remained unnoticed by zoologists until 1957, but is now recognized as a primitive breed brought to the island by Stone Age people at least 6,000 years ago. Its unusual voice (described as a wolf's howl with overtones of whale song!) won it the name of New Guinea Singing Dog. Today endangered in its natural state, it is winning acceptance as an unusual pet.

...and Song Dog

Another ancient breed is the American Indian Dog, whose high-pitched, musical voice has earned it the nickname of the Song Dog. This handsome, coyotelike dog was the hunter and draft animal of the Plains Indians, and its ancestors came from Asia thousands of years ago. Numerous in the 19th century, it was almost extinct in the 1960s when the effort to preserve this historic breed began.

Yellow Dog Dingo

Australia's wild dog, the Dingo is not native to the continent but introduced by man, probably

Conservationists fear that the Dingo may become extinct in the wild within 50 years.

arriving from Asia some 5,000 to 6,000 years ago. Until European settlement in the 18th century, geographical isolation kept the Dingo as one of the last purebred lines of dog. It has survived persecution by farmers, but interbreeding with domestic dogs is even more of a threat; some 80 percent of modern Dingos are thought to be hybrids.

Basenji

A smart little hunting dog, the Basenji *(right)* is North Africa's pariah dog, whose ancient lineage is reflected in Egyptian carvings. Famous as the "barkless dog," like other primitive breeds it has an unusual voice that is described as yodelling. It is said that they were developed without a bark for silent hunting, but in Africa they wear traditional large bells to let their owners hear where they are.

Dixie Dingo

In the 1970s, American biologist Lehr Brisbin, Jr., was struck by how much Carolina's feral dog resembled the Dingo. Recent DNA tests showed that these dogs are indeed "American Dingos," descended from stock brought from Asia by the ancestors of today's Native Americans some 8,000–11,000 years ago. Under the name of Carolina Dog, the "yaller dog" is now taking its place again as a valued companion breed, though it is not yet recognized by the AKC.

HYBRIDS

Crossing the species barrier

Animals of different species can, and sometimes do, interbreed, sometimes through particular circumstances in the wild but more often through human intervention. They must be closely related species, unlike the Hyrcanian dog of Classical myth, said to be produced by crossing dogs with tigers! Domestic dogs can hybridize only with certain members of the canine family such as wolves, coyotes, and jackals.

⚠ *Wolf-dog hybrids are increasingly popular in the U.S. and elsewhere, but they are not a sensible choice for the average pet owner.*

Wolf dogs

Wolves have been deliberately crossed with dogs on many occasions, in an attempt to improve the stock. Today, wolf-dog hybrids may be seen as trendy or macho designer pets. However, dogs have had many generations in which to adapt to living with humans, which wolves have not. Most hybrids inherit the shyer, more reactive temperament of the wolf parent, making them unsuitable household pets.

Saarloos Wolfdog

In the 1920s, Dutch breeder Leendert Saarloos crossed German Shepherd dogs with wolves to create a new breed. He hoped to create tough police dogs, but the wolf's reserve and flight instinct won through. Some succeeded as guide dogs for the blind, but the hectic pace of modern life makes them unsuitable for this role today. Formally recognized in 1972, the Saarloos Wolfdog remains a dog for sensitive and experienced handlers only.

⚠ *The wolf, an animal misunderstood both by admirers who see him as a super-dog and by enemies who see him as a ferocious monster.*

American controversy

In the United States, rapidly growing interest in wolf dogs has brought these animals into the limelight, not always favorably. Inevitably, with an estimated 300,000 wolf dogs in private homes, there have been tragic accidents. The adverse publicity has led to a total ban on these hybrids in several states. Many veterinarians are reluctant to treat them, and even rescue shelters are often unwilling to take them in.

⬆ *Coyote-dog hybrids are less common than wolf dogs, and have the same tendency to inherit the shyer nature of the wild parent.*

Coydogs

Dogs and coyotes can interbreed, although this only occurs in the wild in special circumstances simply because the two species have different social habits and breeding cycles. Many presumed coydogs are now thought to be feral dogs or unusually colored coyotes. Genuine coydogs inherit a mix of characteristics from their parents; a recent study found that most were shy and about 50 percent were fear-biters.

The mythical foxdog

Fox-dog hybrids belong in the realm of folklore; despite countless stories, none has ever been authenticated and most supposed "foxdogs" turn out to be simply dogs with a foxy appearance, not an uncommon type. Dogs and foxes are not sufficiently close relatives to interbreed successfully.

⬆ *The coyote, a species of small wolf, is also known to hybridize with true wolves.*

The day of the jackal

Jackals, however, can interbreed with dogs and produce fertile offspring. In Russia, jackal-Husky hybrids have been bred to work as sniffer dogs, combining the Husky's adaptation to cold climates with the jackal's keen nose. The second-generation hybrids, with one-quarter jackal blood, have proved a great success working at Moscow's Sheremetevo Airport, and are known as Sulimov dogs after their creator Kim Sulimov.

◀◀ *Jackal species, such as this black-backed jackal, have the same chromosome count as dogs, making hybridization possible.*

THE THINGS

DOGS DO

DOGS OF WAR

⬆ *Dogs have played many roles in war, from the Assyrian mastiffs of 650 B.C. (above left) to the German messenger dogs of 1940 (above right).*

The universal soldier

War dogs were high-tech weaponry in ancient times, when huge mastiffs served as attack dogs, guards, message carriers, and draft animals hauling army carts. "Dog soldiers" have continued to serve throughout history, fighting at their masters' sides, tackling rats in the trenches, dragging the wounded to safety, detecting mines, bombs, and ambushes, or simply keeping up morale as treasured mascots.

A hero of Agincourt

In 1415, Sir Piers Legh of Lyme Hall fought at the Battle of Agincourt in northern France, when the English longbowmen of Henry V won their great victory against the French. Hard-pressed by a French soldier, he was saved by the Mastiff bitch that fought by his side. Back in England, this bitch founded the famous line of Lyme Hall Mastiffs that continued into the 19th century.

Canine Conquistadores

In the early 16th century, when Spain conquered the New World, Becerillo was one of the Conquistadores' war Mastiffs, a tool of genocide, trained to kill the natives. Each dog was said to kill 100 men per hour in battle, and they were fed on human flesh, but Becerillo earned the title of *perro sabio,* "learned dog," for capturing fugitives unharmed and sparing an old woman who knelt to him.

Prisoner of war

Judy the Pointer was a Royal Navy mascot that served on a gunboat in World War II. Torpedoed and captured by the Japanese, she and the

Judy wearing her Dickin ⏵ Medal, the Animals' VC.

crew spent two years as prisoners of war in appalling conditions. There she did her best to defend her fellow captives from the prison guards and kept up morale with her courage and endurance. Liberated in 1945, she came home to Britain as a national heroine.

Parachute hero

Rob was a working farm dog in Shropshire, England, until 1942, when he was enlisted as a war dog. An outstanding patrol dog, he graduated to working as a "paradog" with the SAS, making more than 20 solo parachute drops into enemy territory in North Africa and

Rob's eight awards included the Dickin Medal (above) and RSPCA silver medal "For Valour."

Italy. Decorated with more military awards than any other animal in British history, he returned home after the war to live out his life on the farm.

A gallant mascot

In 1941 the Royal Rifles of Canada, defending

Hong Kong from the Japanese, were amply seconded by their regimental mascot, Gander the Newfoundland. The massive dog defended his companions gallantly. His last act was to snatch up a hand grenade thrown at his friends and carry it away from them, saving their lives at the cost of his own. Belatedly, in 2000, he was awarded the Dickin Medal, the "Animals' VC."

The dogs of Vietnam

The 4,000 dogs that served in the Vietnam War (1957–1975) are credited with saving the lives of 10,000 American servicemen. Tragically, at the end of the war they were classified as surplus equipment and euthanized or abandoned: despite the pleas of their handlers, a mere 250 war dogs made it back to the United States. Since the 1990s, Vietnam veterans and others have campaigned to raise war dog memorials across the United States.

In 1994 a memorial was dedicated at the U.S. Marine Corps War Dog Cemetery on Guam to honor the 25 Doberman Pinschers that died in the Battle of Guam in 1944.

SEADOGS

Iron lady

Peggy, mascot of the battleship HMS *Iron Duke*, joined up in 1915 as a puppy and served on board throughout World War I, receiving a medal for her attendance in 1916 at Jutland, the greatest naval battle of the war. Retired to shore life in 1919, she was later auctioned for charity (raising 135 guineas for St. Bartholomew's Hospital) and was overjoyed to be presented back to the *Iron Duke*, where she spent the rest of her life.

Newfoundland hero

When the SS *Ethie* ran aground off the west coast of Newfoundland in 1919, the 92 people aboard were saved by a dog that swam out to bring a line ashore. He was presented with a special collar and medal for bravery. In 2000, the collar was rediscovered and presented to the Newfoundland Museum at a ceremony attended by Hilda Menchions who, as a baby aboard the *Ethie*, owed her life to the brave dog.

Today, Newfoundland heroes still save lives ▶▶ at sea. Indeed, there are now nautical rescue training schools where dogs learn the techniques of water lifesaving, including leaping to the rescue from a helicopter when access by boat is too dangerous.

Lucky terrier

A Jack Russell called Bundy was proclaimed "Australia's luckiest dog" after he was plucked from the sea 2 miles (3 km) offshore in Port Phillip Bay. Water police failed to find him after he jumped from his master's boat, but he managed to keep afloat for 45 minutes in rough seas until he was spotted by a passing powerboat and rescued. His relieved owner swore that Bundy would wear a life jacket next time he went to sea.

Most dogs love the sea, and many breeds have a long history of working with sailors.

Cuddly memento

Another Bulldog naval hero was Joey, who started out in 1915 as the pet of the chaplain to Portsmouth Dockyard but later became mascot of HMS *Renown* and companion of Admiral Sir David Beatty. He saw plenty of action, including the Battles of Jutland and Heligoland. In 1922, his heroic naval career was commemorated when he was reproduced as a soft toy made of velvet and seated on a white ensign.

Not just a nuisance…

A Great Dane named Just Nuisance was classed as Able Seaman although he never went to sea. Based in Simonstown, South Africa, Nuisance, was so persistent in attaching himself to sailors that in 1939, the Navy gave in and enlisted him. Renowned for the care he showed for his sailor friends, he became a legend in Simonstown, where today his statue watches over the town square.

Fishermen's friend

The Portuguese Water Dog was developed by fishermen as a working crew member. At sea the dogs could retrieve anything that fell overboard, carry messages between boats or from boat to shore, and swim out with fishing floats; ashore, they guarded the boats, nets, and catch. Modern technology has replaced them on fishing boats, but today, these sturdy, intelligent dogs have moved on to activities such as agility and water trials.

Scottish favorite

Ship's dog of the Norwegian minesweeper *Thorodd* in World War II, Bamse the St. Bernard earned a PDSA award for courage during action. Stationed at the Scottish town of Montrose in 1942, he made himself responsible for collecting shipmates from the pubs at closing time, and everyone came to know him. Upon his death in 1944, local schools closed to allow hundreds of children to attend his funeral. Today, his grave is still honored in Montrose.

▲ *Harriet the St. Bernard and men of the Norwegian submarine* Utvaer *attend a 60th-anniversary ceremony at Bamse's grave.*

MASCOTS

University dog

One of America's best-loved university mascots is Uga, sixth in a line of solid white English Bulldogs that began with Uga I in 1956. Dressed in his red football jersey, Uga attends every game of the university football team, the Georgia Bulldogs. Uga V, father of the current incumbent, was featured in Clint Eastwood's film *Midnight in the Garden of Good and Evil*, playing the part of his own father, Uga IV.

Victorian hero

When the 2nd Battalion of the 66th Royal Berkshire Regiment fought at the Battle of Maiwand in 1880 during the Second Afghan War, one of the few survivors was the Regiment's dog, a brown and white mongrel named Bobbie. Later, the little dog was present at Osborne House on the Isle of Wight when Queen Victoria presented Gallantry medals to the survivors.

◄◄ *Today Bobbie is on display in the Regimental museum in Salisbury, England.*

American hero

Stubby, a Bull Terrier mix, progressed from stray to army mascot to World War I hero, to end up the most decorated war dog in American history. Accompanying the 102nd Infantry to France, he participated in 17 battles, warned of mustard gas attacks, located wounded soldiers, and even caught a German spy. He returned home to national acclaim—and promotion to the rank of honorary sergeant.

▲ *In 1945, Smoky became an "unoffical war dog" after carrying communication cable through a pipe to help protect planes and ground crew.*

The littlest soldier

Among the many heroic mascots of World War II, Smoky the Yorkshire Terrier earned a special place as "the littlest war dog." An American Army/Air Force mascot, she flew on 12 combat missions, was awarded eight battle stars, and was named "Champion Mascot of the Southwest Pacific Area in 1944." More than just a mascot, she was also the first Therapy Dog on record, visiting wounded soldiers in hospital in America and overseas.

Secret society mascot

The Chinese Foo Dog, a cousin of the Chow Chow, is the mascot of the Tongs—China's ancient secret society, said to be the oldest secret cult in the world. Tong members kept these dogs as a symbol of their organization, and they are considered to bring good fortune. However, the breed is not universally recognized.

His Master's Voice

Less a mascot than an icon, Nipper *(right)* the terrier is known to music lovers worldwide as the symbol of HMV and the EMI record label.

Master's Voice. The original version featured a phonograph, not a gramophone, but failed to sell because "Dogs don't listen to phonographs!"

Nipper (so named because he nipped visitors) was born in Bristol in 1884 and died three years before his master Francis Barraud painted *His*

⩔ *Titina, a terrier, traveled as mascot with explorer General Umberto Nobile in the dirigible* Italia *on the ill-fated 1928 Italian expedition to the North Pole.*

⩘ *Modern fire engines no longer use Dalmatians to run ahead clearing the way, but many firehouses still keep Dalmatian mascots.*

Firehouse dogs

In the days of horse-drawn fire engines, most American firehouses kept Dalmatians not only to guard their horses and equipment but to run ahead of the firefighters, clearing the way. The men prided themselves on the shining paint and polished brass of their firecarts, and handsome coach dogs added to the effect. Today, fire departments across the United States keep the tradition alive with much-loved Dalmatian mascots.

ROYAL DOGS

Many centuries before Pugs became favorites with European rulers, they were the companions of Chinese emperors—truly royal dogs.

Orange Pugs

When Spanish troops attacked the camp of Dutch prince William the Silent in 1572, his Pug dog Pompey raised the alarm and saved his master. Thereafter, Pugs became the symbol of the royal House of Orange, and Dutch royalists bedecked them with orange ribbons. When William and Mary of Orange came to the English throne in 1689, they brought their Pugs, which soon achieved popularity in England.

On the scaffold

In 1587, the executioner of Mary Queen of Scots discovered, after he had carried out his grim task, that the beloved lapdog that shared her cell had hidden under her skirts to go with her to the scaffold. Touched by the dog's refusal to leave his mistress's body, despite the decree that no mementos of Mary should be kept, he smuggled her faithful companion out to be adopted by one of the Queen's ladies.

Canine cavalier

A Cavalier hero of the English Civil War was Prince Rupert of the Rhine's white Poodle, Boy. The Roundheads claimed Boy, the first poodle seen in England, was Rupert's familiar spirit—weapon-proof, and able to speak, prophesy, and become invisible. They rejoiced when Boy fell at the Battle of Marston Moor in 1644, believing Rupert to be lost without his pet demon—and indeed, Marston Moor saw the end of his success.

Frederick the Great

Frederick II of Prussia (1712–1786) favored the daintiest of lapdogs—Italian Greyhounds, which accompanied him everywhere. He took great care of them; his military greatcoat was specially tailored to allow him to tuck a dog inside to keep it warm, and on his deathbed, his last words were a request to an aide to wrap a quilt around his dog. It was Frederick who coined the phrase, "The more I see of men, the more I love my dogs."

Inseparable from his dogs, Frederick was buried beside his favorites. ▶▶

Landseer's painting of ▶▶ Queen Victoria at Osborne in 1865 includes not only a favorite horse but two of her beloved dogs.

Victorian favorite

Queen Victoria filled her life with dogs of all shapes and sizes, but the toy spaniel Dash, the dog of her childhood, was special. Indeed, the Queen's first action after her coronation was to go home and bathe Dash! His portrait became a popular theme for Victorian embroideresses. When he died in 1840, his epitaph read, "Attachment without selfishness, Playfulness without malice, and Fidelity without deceit."

Russian survivor

When the Czar of Russia and his family were executed in 1918, his daughter Anastasia was clutching her favorite dog, Jimmy, a King Charles Spaniel. He died with his mistress, and was buried in the same pit. There was one survivor of the Russian royal family, the Czarevitch's Springer Spaniel, Joy, who was rescued by a Russian guard and is said to have ended his days in England with a British officer.

Joy the spaniel attends his master the ▶▶ young Czarevitch in this portrait of the Russian royal family, taken in about 1914.

Her Majesty's heelers

Pembroke Corgis have become part of the popular image of Queen Elizabeth II since she acquired her first, Dookie, in 1933, when she was seven years old. Today's royal pack descend from Susan, an 18th birthday present, who died in 1959. Not everyone shares the Queen's affection for them: Corgis were bred to drive cattle by nipping their heels, and the royal dogs have a reputation for nipping sentries and visitors.

WHITE HOUSE DOGS

Admirable Airedale

The American public has always appreciated the dogs of the White House. In the case of one of the least popular presidents, Warren Harding (president from 1921–1923), his Airedale Terrier, Laddie Boy, received more press attention than his master. After Harding's death, the Newsboys' Association resolved on a monument to his dog and 19,134 newsboys donated a penny each to be melted down and cast into a statue of Laddie Boy.

🔺 *Checkers the Cocker Spaniel, famous as "the dog that saved Nixon's career," remained a much-loved member of the Nixon family until his death in 1964.*

The Checkers speech

In 1952, future U.S. President Richard Nixon scotched tales of corruption with his famous "Checkers' speech." The only gift he had accepted, he said, was "a little black-and-white Cocker Spaniel puppy. My daughter had named it Checkers… I said that regardless of what anyone said about it, I was going to keep it." American dog-lovers promptly voted him in as vice president, and Checkers remained.

A special Scottie

Franklin Delano Roosevelt (president 1933–1945) introduced perhaps the White House's best-loved canine resident in Fala the Scottish Terrier. Fala and his master were inseparable, which led to a major scandal in 1944 when the president was falsely accused of sending a destroyer, at vast expense, to pick up his dog. The Scottie became the only dog to be honored with a statue *(above)* at a presidential memorial.

From Russia with love

John Fitzgerald Kennedy (president 1961–1963) and his family filled the White House with animals, including numerous dogs. One of the most notable was Pushinka, a gift to Kennedy's daughter from Nikita Khrushchev and the daughter of Strelka, one of the first dogs in space. Pushinka went on to confirm the entente cordiale between Russia and the United States by producing a litter of puppies sired by Kennedy's Welsh Terrier Charlie.

The ear incident

Lyndon B. Johnson (president 1963–1969) was less politically adept with his two Beagles, Him and Her. When he picked the dogs up by their ears at a photographic session in 1964, dog-lovers were outraged—and Johnson didn't help matters by his unapologetic attitude. He did it, he said, "to make them bark—it's good for them!" Later, a white mongrel named Yuki fared better and was allowed to attend cabinet meetings.

Publicity hound

Millie, the Springer Spaniel of George Bush (president 1989–1993) not only received her fair share of media attention but augmented it with an "autobiography," *Millie's Book*, courtesy of Barbara Bush. Uniquely among First Dogs, she

⬆ *Barney was presented to George W. Bush by the governor of New Jersey, and became one of the most popular First Dogs.*

was also the mother of one of her successors. The litter of puppies she produced in the White House included Spot, later to become famous as President George W. Bush's dog.

Spot and Scots

Nothing if not a traditionalist when it comes to dogs, President George W. Bush (president 2001–) started out with Spot the Springer Spaniel and, with Barney the Scottie, reintroduced Scottish Terriers to the White House. The well-behaved Barney proved such a success that he was joined in 2005 by a second Scottie, Miss Beazley. The famous Fala would no doubt approve!

⬇ *Lyndon Johnson came to regret posing with his two Beagles at the infamous photoshoot.*

AMAZING JOURNEYS

From Pole to Pole

Bothie, the Jack Russell, mascot to the 1979 Transglobe Expedition, was the only dog to visit both North and South Poles. Equipped against the polar chill with a specially made coat, body stockings, sweater, knit cap, and padded booties, Bothie kept his human companions' spirits up on the demanding adventure, and was allowed to rest at base camp while they trekked across the ice. On his return in 1982, he was feted on television, and voted Pet of the Year.

⬆ *Bothie's achievement will remain unique, as dogs are now banned from the Antarctic.*

The first astronaut

In 1957, Russian Husky bitch Laika made history as the first "earthling" to travel in space, when she was launched as a passenger in the Soviet satellite Sputnik II. Her voyage enabled Soviet scientists to study the effects of space travel so that human astronauts might follow her. But they had not yet developed

A stray plucked from ▶▶
the Moscow streets,
Laika became a victim
of the space race.

the technology to bring her capsule back to earth. She died in space when her oxygen supply ran out ten days later.

Channel hopping

In 1914, when his owner James Brown was posted to France with the North Staffordshire Regiment, his Collie/Irish Terrier cross Prince achieved the incredible feat of tracing him to the French trenches. How he crossed the Channel remains a mystery. He was adopted by the regiment and spent the duration of the war with them, undertaking valuable service as a ratter. After the war he returned to England with his master.

Up, up, and away

In 1784, a favorite lapdog accompanied Italian aeronaut Vicenzo Lunardi on the first hydrogen balloon ascent in England. At peak height, the little dog was frozen. As the press reported, "had not Mr. Lunardi's regard for his dog led him to afford it the warmth of his bosom, the animal would inevitably have perished." A cat that accompanied them received less consideration and was jettisoned, but luckily survived his fall.

Long-distance runners

From the 17th century, Dalmatians were popular coach dogs, running behind (or even under) smart carriages as a

Originally guards to repel ▸▸ highwaymen, coach dogs were later viewed as vital fashion accessories.

fashionable escort and guard. They had to be superbly fit. In 1851, one dog followed the London to Brighton coach on eight successive days— 74 miles (120 km) each way. This same dog once escorted a coach that went to Tunbridge Wells instead. When the coach stopped at Tunbridge Wells, the Dalmatian took the road to Brighton on his own, returning to London with the next London coach.

before being dropped. Although she needed two operations for her injuries, she survived to tell the tale. Her owner refused to blame the bird, a protected species, and the American public rallied to help pay her veterinary bills.

Uncomfortable car ride

In 2005, an Irish dog survived a 50-mile (81-km) journey stuck on the hood of a car as it sped down the highway. The motorist had heard a bump as he was driving along, but it was only when he arrived at Belfast that he heard barking and discovered a black-and-white Collie cross trapped in the radiator grille. A veterinarian reported that he had no major injuries, but was understandably slightly grumpy.

High-flying Dachshund

Ava the Dachshund took an unusual, and uncomfortable, flight in 2002, when she was snatched from her home in Maine by a bald eagle and carried 300 feet (91 m) up in the air

HOMING INSTINCT

American hero

In the 1920s, a Collie named Bobbie achieved fame when, after being lost in Indiana, he found his way home six months later to Silverton, Oregon. His journey took him six months. Sightings of him on his marathon trek helped admirers to plot his 3,000-mile (4,800-km) route across major rivers, the Great Plains, and the Rocky Mountains. He was awarded a gold collar, medals, and his own model bungalow, and enjoyed a further 12 years of peaceful home life.

⤒ *Silverton, Oregon, honors its most famous canine citizen Bobbie the homing Collie with this Water Street mural by artist Lori Webb.*

Russian marathon

When Russian engineer Viktor Strupovets moved from his home in the Urals to Belarus in 1979, he had to leave Vesna, his German Shepherd Dog, behind with friends since dogs were not allowed in his new apartment. Vesna did not settle, and finally broke her chain and disappeared. An incredible four years later she appeared at Viktor's side. After her 1,100-mile (1,770-km) journey, she was allowed to remain with him.

Sailing home

In the 19th century, a Collie was sent from Inverkeithing, Scotland, to his new owner in Calcutta. Shortly after his arrival in India, he disappeared, and a few months later bounded into his old home in Scotland. Apparently he had stowed away on a homebound ship, disembarked at Dundee, and then boarded a coastal vessel to take him to his home port.

Loyal Lhasa

Even little dogs have achieved astonishing homing feats. In 1983, Paula Kerslake took her Lhasa Apso, Anni Fanni, to stay with a relative in Apple Valley, California, hoping the desert climate would put an end to Anni's flea infestation. Two months later, Anni found her way home—a 100-mile (160-km) journey. Oh, and she brought her fleas home too.

Overboard and overland

The owners of Spook, a German Shepherd Dog, were en route from California to a new home in Alaska in 1976 when their pet was lost overboard off British Columbia. Seven months later, visiting their old home in California, they found Spook in the local dog pound, worn out after tramping 1,000 miles (1,600 km) home. Due to be put down as a stray the next day, instead, Spook headed for his new home in Alaska with his overjoyed owners.

↥ *The stars of* Homeward Bound II*: an American Bulldog, a Golden Retriever, and a Siamese cat.*

Best-seller

Real-life journeys like these inspired Sheila Burnford to write her best-selling novel *The Incredible Journey* (1961) in which two dogs and a Siamese cat travel 250 miles (400 km) through the Canadian wilderness to find their family. The much-loved book inspired three films, *The Incredible Journey* (1963), *Homeward Bound: The Incredible Journey* (1993), and *Homeward Bound II: Lost in San Francisco* (1996).

Lost in the desert

Nick, a German Shepherd bitch, was lost in the Arizona desert while on a camping trip with her owner Doug Simpson. After searching for her for two weeks, Simpson had to give up and return to his home in Washington. Four months later, Nick joined him. She was gaunt and weary—hardly surprisingly, after a 2,000-mile (3,200-km) journey across desert, mountains, and the Grand Canyon.

↥ *In 1812, a dog named Moffino accompanied his master, a Milanese corporal, on Napoleon's Russian campaign. Separated from his owner, Moffino made his own way across Europe and amazed everyone when he arrived back home in Italy.*

SNIFFER DOGS

Tracker dogs

The earliest use humans made of the dog's sense of smell was for tracking—first helping hunters to find game, and since ancient times also to follow human trails, seeking criminals, outlaws, or lost people. In the Middle Ages it is recorded how Scottish heroes Robert the Bruce and William Wallace were tracked by "sleuth-hounds," and today, the police still depend upon tracker dogs to follow a trail.

▲ *An American firefighter with canine assistants, trained to sniff out the origins of a blaze.*

September 11 heroes

When disaster strikes, search and rescue dogs, trained to locate victims, are invaluable. After the 2001 attack on the World Trade Center, more than 300 dogs from all over America joined NYPD canine units in searching the 16-acre (6.5-Ha) disaster site for survivors. On behalf of them all, police dog Apollo was nominated to receive the PDSA Dickin Medal "for tireless courage in the service of humanity."

Truffle dogs

Gourmets pay huge prices for truffles, but these underground fungi take some finding. This led to the development, centuries ago, of perhaps the earliest specialized sniffer dog—the truffle dog. In the 19th century, it was said that a good dog earned enough in the truffle season to support a family of 12. Today, top truffle dogs are so valued that they are sometimes kidnapped and held for ransom.

Avalanche aid

Human rescuers have trouble locating avalanche victims buried under snow, but trained Avalanche Rescue dogs can sniff them out. The training takes three years, but has proved its worth. In the time it takes 20 humans to check an area with probe poles, one dog can cover eight times that area, and more thoroughly, often making all the difference between a body recovery and the recovery of a live person.

▼ *Avalanche dogs can detect human victims buried under up to 13 feet (4 m) of snow.*

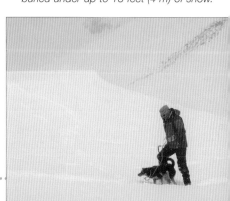

Tangle the Cocker Spaniel has proved more efficient at detecting bladder cancer from human urine samples than any technology.

Doctor dogs

The dog's nose can even detect human ailments. Scientists have found that dogs can identify the smell of cancer. In one case George, a Standard Schnauzer trained in Florida to detect melanomas, persisted in pointing out a mole that three doctors and two biopsies had showed to be noncancerous. This prompted further investigation and saved the patient's life—George was right and the other experts were wrong.

Sniffing out arson

How do you tell when a fire was caused by accident or by arson? Ask a dog! Fire investigation dogs search fire sites for accelerants such as paraffin and paint thinner more efficiently and faster than humans or technical electronic field equipment. Since Mattie, a black Labrador, was trained for Connecticut State Police in the 1980s, hundreds of dogs have taken up employment in this field.

Conservation dogs

Most dog owners object to their pets sniffing feces, but conservation dogs are encouraged to do this! Trained to identify the scats of a particular species, they enable biologists to study endangered animals more cheaply and safely than techniques such as radio collaring. One New England study of Right Whales even employed detector dogs to locate floating whale scat from boats.

Sniffing out bodies

Finding dead bodies is another task where sniffer dogs excel over human searchers. Search and rescue dogs trained to locate live victims become distressed if they only find bodies, so special "cadaver dogs" are trained to detect corpses or even corpse traces, underground or underwater. To take just one example, Zeus, a German Shepherd, located a body wrapped in plastic and buried under concrete four years earlier!

Search and rescue dogs may use ground or airborne scent to locate disaster victims.

ASSISTANCE DOGS

Helping the blind

Some blind people have trained dogs to lead them around since Roman times (as shown by a wall painting at Pompeii), but it took World War I to show us the value of guide dogs. In the early 1920s, the number of soldiers blinded in the war led to the establishment of the first formal training schools for "Seeing Eye" dogs in Germany and Switzerland. These proved so successful that guide dogs are now valued worldwide.

Many breeds have proved suitable guide ☀ dogs, but today Labradors and Labrador-Golden Retriever crosses are favorites.

First Lady of the Seeing Eye

In 1929, Morris Frank, a blind insurance salesman from Tennessee, traveled to Switzerland to become the first American owner of a "Seeing Eye" dog. He was paired with a German Shepherd bitch named Kiss, a name he quickly changed to Buddy. Back in the United States, she achieved fame as the "First Lady of the Seeing Eye," transformed Frank's life, and inspired the foundation in 1920 of The Seeing Eye Guide Dog School.

Guide dog's marathon

North America's Appalachian Trail is one of the most perilous mountain routes in the world. Completing the 2,175-mile (3,500-km) trail over peaks and rivers across 14 states is a feat of endurance. For Bill Irwin, who is blind, it might have seemed impossible, but with the aid of his German Shepherd guide dog, despite storms and blizzards, he completed the nine-month hike successfully.

Helping the deaf

A later, but equally valuable development was the training of Hearing Ear dogs for the deaf. Hearing Dogs alert their owners to everyday sounds from doorbells to crying babies, and also use their initiative to respond to unexpected noises and events. Deafness can be very isolating, and Hearing Dogs also help their owners to enjoy a wider social life and to function at work in the hearing world.

Tiny hero

Bentley, a little terrier cross that works as Hearing Dog for his deaf owner Colin James of Bournemouth, was awarded the title of Heroic Hearing Dog of the Year for 2005. At irregular intervals, his

Bella the service dog carries items such as ☀ packages or phone for her disabled owner.

DOG BIZ

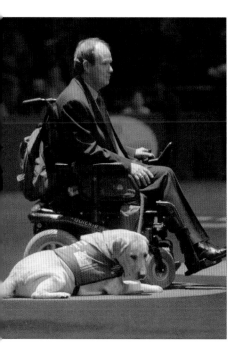

◀◀ *Endal the Labrador helps his partner Allen Parton cope with the hidden disability of memory loss as well as with practical tasks.*

Dog of the Millennium

Endal, a yellow Labrador, was named Dog of the Millennium for his feats as assistance dog of wheelchair-bound Allen Parton. A road accident had left Parton without memory, speech, or emotions, wanting only to die. Endal not only acts as his partner's arms and legs (even teaching himself to use a cash machine), but helped him to speak and feel again. Today they are famous as ambassadors for Canine Partners for Independence.

Seizure alert dogs

Specialized assistance dogs can also turn around the lives of epilepsy sufferers. Seizure alert dogs are trained to detect the signs of an imminent seizure long before any human could do so (20 to 45 minutes beforehand) and to warn their owners, giving them time to get to a place of safety. Having a reliable warning system enables epileptics to lead a normal life without taking undue risks.

master's heart stops beating while he is asleep and he stops breathing, but Bentley is a lifesaver, alerting Mrs. James whenever this happens. He also fetched help to an elderly dog who was choking, saving her life, too.

Helping the disabled

Assistance dogs, trained to help disabled people, can carry out tasks such as picking up dropped items, opening and closing doors, helping owners to dress and undress, and even loading and unloading the washing machine. They are also trained lifesavers, able to push an unconscious person into the recovery position before summoning help, and are expected to use their initiative to react to unexpected crises.

▲ *Chris Rupert's service dog carries items she needs ready at hand in his backpack.*

LAW AND ORDER

Trailblazer

The first recorded use of a dog trained for law enforcement occurred in 1816, when a Revenue Officer's Bull Terrier helped to arrest a party of Scottish whiskey smugglers. The dog was taught to grab suspects' horses by the nose so they spilled their loads, a far cry from the gentler tactics of modern Revenue dogs!

⬆ *Police dogs are invaluable for crowd control, like this K-9 unit helping to keep the peace at an antiwar protest in Chicago in 2003.*

Because of the Belgians...

The world's first police dog service started in Ghent, Belgium, in the 1890s. Unable to afford the extra men they needed, the Ghent police tried dogs, and were amazed at how valuable the first "dog watchmen" proved to be. In 1899, the Gent Hondenbrigade was formally founded, and proved so successful that police forces around the world followed suit.

Dogged pursuit

In 1999, an off-duty policeman in Northumbria, England, was walking his police dog Carl, a German Shepherd, when they spotted a burgled shop. Carl pursued the scent of the robbers for 8 miles (13 km), crossing two 8-foot (2.4-m) walls, a tall fence, and a river. While the officer thought the pursuit hopeless, Carl was unstoppable and five hours later he caught the robbers napping at a railroad station.

Faking it

Dogs are invaluable in assisting with arrests, as two Oklahoma police officers realized when they were chasing a suspect who looked like he was getting away. In an imaginative bluff, one officer imitated barks and growls while the other threatened to release his dog. The suspect hastily surrendered. As they handcuffed him, he kept worrying, "Where's the dog?"—only to be told "There's no dog, buddy!"

Noses for hire

Two sniffer dogs working for the English South Yorkshire Police command a fee of over $1,800 per day when hired out to assist other forces. Eddie the Springer Spaniel and Jake the Border Collie underwent special training to work as Victim Recovery Dogs. Their work ranges from

Cadaver dogs assist the police by sniffing out ▸▸ bodies, even drowned victims underwater.

locating bodies to detecting microscopic traces of blood or human remains—often enough, in the age of DNA testing, to solve a case.

Three-legged police dog

Another dog that didn't let physical problems stop him from working is Snoopy, a Springer Spaniel employed by Wiltshire Constabulary in England, to sniff out drugs, firearms, and ammunition. An infected injury meant he had to have a hindleg amputated, but the seven-year-old dog was back on the force, with only three legs, a mere two months later.

countless arrests, made more than 200 drug finds, and was stabbed, shot at, and even poisoned, but survived to enjoy retirement at his ex-handler's home.

▼ *A trainer with a padded sleeve teaches a police dog how to tackle armed suspects.*

Shortly after losing a leg, Snoopy was back on the job, detecting two substantial drug caches.

Lexington legend

A German Shepherd Dog from North Carolina is the only dog to win two North American Police Dog Work Association's Medals of Honor, both for saving officers' lives by tackling armed suspects. In his 10-year career, he assisted in

DOGS OF ALL TRADES

Official greeter

Patsy Ann, a Bull Terrier, made herself the "Official Greeter of Juneau, Alaska," in the 1930s. One of the town's most popular residents, she insisted on greeting every ship that docked at the harbor, sensing their approach long before they came into sight, even though she was deaf from birth. Today, tourists are welcomed at the docks by her bronze memorial statue.

⬆ *A canine admirer beside Patsy Ann's statue at Juneau docks, erected in 1992 as a 50th anniversary tribute.*

Crown Jewels guardian

In the 1920s, a small mongrel named Monty helped to guard the Crown Jewels at the Tower of London *(right)*. The curator's pet (and a tourist attraction in his own right), he earned his keep when he found the flaw in a new security system, demonstrating that a dog (and therefore a burglar) could pass under the detector beams without setting off the alarm. The system was hastily adjusted.

London firemen's dog

In 1833, London's first fire brigade was staffed by Thames watermen—and their dog. Chance the Bull Terrier, rescued from the Thames after his owner threw him in with a brick tied to his neck, became a London legend as he led the horse-drawn fire engines to fires. He was painted by several artists and presented with a brass collar. In old age he died under the wheels of one of his beloved fire engines.

Artist's model

The Weimaraners of American art photographer William Wegman are famed for their extraordinary poses in his soulful compositions. It all began in 1970 when the first of the clan, Man Ray, objected to being left out of his master's work in the photographic studio. He, and his successors Fay Wray and her descendants, proved such talented models that they now appear everywhere from T-shirts to children's books.

Prison worker

Tally the Boxer started work at Arbour Hill prison in Dublin in 2002, not as a law enforcer but to cheer up the inmates. Prison staff were inspired to employ Tally after an officer brought in a stray puppy he found on his way to work. Staff and prisoners

DOG BIZ

Tally the Boxer—a welfare worker with a difference at Arbour Hill Prison in Dublin.

alike were so upset when her owners came to claim her that they decided to adopt Tally to improve the quality of prison life.

Charity collectors

In 1882, Help the Collie started work as a charity collector at Brighton Railway Station, Sussex, England. His nine-year career raising funds for railroadmen's orphans was so successful that other English railroads trained similar dogs. One of the last, London Jack V, raised over $7,000 between 1923 and his death in 1931. Today, mounted on display in a glass case, he continues to raise funds at the Bluebell Railway, Sussex.

Umbrella business

A Victorian account tells of a retriever named Shock who lived with his owners in Arundel, England. On days when it looked like rain, Shock would gather up umbrellas and walk down to the railroad station with them. Grateful passengers paid him a halfpenny each for his trouble, and Shock would then carry his earnings to the grocery store and exchange them for biscuits.

⬆ *London Jack V at work on Waterloo Station, photographed with friends in 1925.*

UNUSUAL EMPLOYMENT

Beagle artists

A team of Beagles in Newfoundland raise funds for charity by painting pictures. Trainer Tonji Stewart used clicker training to teach Piper and Tuig to daub paint on canvas with a painting mitten worn on one paw. Their colorful abstracts are selling well, and the dogs thoroughly enjoy their artistic career, even though Tuig has been almost totally blind from birth and has never seen his own artwork.

⋆ A guide dog with a difference, Pippin leads the way for her blind friends Lotty and Dotty.

⋆ Learning new skills through clicker training made life more fun for blind Tuig. As well as painting (above), he can also ride a tricycle!

Mobile walking frame

Hariel the Pyrenean Mountain Dog is the first of his breed to become a "mobile walking frame" in Britain. His 70-year-old owner ignored advice that Pyreneans were unsuited to training to help the disabled (although they have been used successfully in the U.S.), and trained him herself to help her stand up, walk beside her so she can lean on him, and catch her when she loses her balance.

Rock musician

Not many rock stars pluck their guitar strings with their teeth, but Sven, half of the team that made up the acid rock band K-9 Fusion, didn't have much choice—he was a dog. The talented mongrel provided vocals, guitar, electric bass, and piano on the band's debut CD, with owner Steve Brooks on the drums and backing vocals coming from an assortment of Sven's canine friends.

Epilepsy alert

Seiko, a handsome black Standard Poodle, became Canada's first seizure dog when he was trained to watch over epileptic Sue Hoffman. Seiko was taught exactly what to do if she suffered a seizure, from dragging her away from traffic to sounding an emergency alert at home. Not content with that, he taught himself to predict seizures before they happened, enabling his owner to lead a near-normal life.

Vineyard helper

Tomi, a yellow Labrador who lives with a wine-maker in Marlborough, New Zealand, has a nose for grapes. Most vineyards rely on laboratories to gauge when the grapes are ready for harvesting, but Tomi has proved

Most vineyards rely on technology to determine the optimum time to harvest grapes, but Tomi the Labrador proves that a dog's nose is just as efficient as the most high-tech instrument.

herself just as accurate. She had been helping herself to the pick of the crop before her talent was discovered, but now her owner knows that when she starts grabbing grapes, it's time to harvest them.

Night watchman

Neville sleeps most of the day because he works night shifts. The scruffy little terrier is

trained to watch over the sleep of 13-year-old Brooke Kelly of Sydney, Australia, whose rare genetic disorder means she risks dying in her sleep when she stops breathing. With Neville, one of the first two dogs in the world trained for this purpose, there to raise the alarm, she can go to bed without worrying.

Airfield assistants

In the U.S., unwanted Border Collies are finding new careers clearing airfields of geese to reduce the risk of bird strike, a real hazard to aircraft. Border Collie Rescue, which trains and supplies the dogs, reckons that only 5–10 percent of the dogs coming into rescue are suited to this specialized work. Those that make the grade save lives as well as damage to planes, and have a wonderful time chasing birds for a living.

▼ *Border Collies also employ their herding skills to clear geese from parks and golf courses. A planned pattern of harassment, rather than random chasing, is required to persuade the flocks to relocate.*

TALENTED DOGS

Type-setter

Arli, an English setter, belonging to Elizabeth Mann Borgese, learned to use a specially adapted typewriter with oversize keys that he could operate with his nose, from simple phrases like "go car" and "a good dog," he graduated to stating his wishes, as in "dog get ball and go bee beeb bed." Some of his typings were published as Arli's Poems, described as "collaborations" between Arli and his owner.

▲ *In the early 19th century, Munito the French Poodle enthralled audiences by performing mathematical feats with numbered cards.*

Mathematical mongrel

Chris, a Beagle cross from Rhode Island, became famous in the 1950s as "the Mathematical Mongrel" as he tapped out correct answers to sums with his paw. He went on to learn the alphabet (one tap for A, two for B, etc.) to answer questions, even predicting the winner of a horse race. When asked how he produced his predictions and calculations, he answered simply, "Smart dog!"

Skateboard stunts

In California, Tyson the Bulldog *(above)* watched his human family skateboarding, and decided to join them. He quickly worked out how to run along on three legs while steering his board with the fourth, jumping aboard as soon as it picked up speed, and is now a passionate skater. His owners report that a typical skateboarding session for Tyson can last as long as two hours, and cover 2 miles (4 km).

Canine clairvoyant

In the 1960s Missie, a Boston Terrier from Denver, astounded the world with her psychic powers. Barking her answers to questions, she was rarely wrong. Skeptics boggled when she barked out their Social Security numbers, unlisted telephone numbers, and even the serial numbers of dollars in their wallets. She also predicted national and international events—and the exact time of her own death.

Surfing stunts

When former international surfer Peter Bounds adopted a stray dog that turned up on his doorstep in west Wales, he found a kindred

DOG BIZ

▲ *Who needs a wetsuit? Max is in his element surfing at Pembrokeshire, England.*

spirit. Not content with hanging around his new owner's water sports center, Max wanted to join in. After trying out a surfboard, he took to the hobby like a duck to water and is now an enthusiastic surfer that refuses to be left behind.

Brain of Britain

American psychologist Stanley Coren classifies Border Collies as the cleverest breed of dog,

▼ *Britain's brainiest dog, Benjamin, shows off his well-earned collection of toys.*

ranking top out of 133 breeds for brainpower and obedience. In 2004, reporters hailed Benjamin, a Border Collie from Dorset, as the brainiest dog in Britain when they discovered that he knows 56 favorite toys by name (including "stegosaurus" and "guanodon") and takes a mere four minutes to learn the name of a new toy.

Bellringer

A 19th-century convent in France served food daily to 20 paupers, each of whom rang a bell outside on arrival and his portion was then passed out. The convent dog watched this with interest and followed suit. When the convent realized that an extra meal was being collected each day and identified the culprit, they were so impressed with the dog's ingenuity that they allowed him to continue.

Pharie, mascot of Cologne Football Stadium, isn't content just to look the part, but also displays his riding skills on a toy motorcycle. ▲

Weather forecaster

In September 1938, William Montgomery was about to launch his fishing boat off the New England coast when his dog Redsey refused to come aboard and stood on the dock barking. This was so unlike Redsey that he felt he couldn't ignore it, so he stayed ashore. An hour later the dog was proved right when a hurricane hit the coast, smashing boats and killing more than 600 people.

DOGS IN SPORT

Pride of Ireland

In the late 1860s, a small black Greyhound named Master McGrath was "the pride of all Ireland" as the greatest coursing dog of all time. His skill and courage made him almost unbeaten at hare coursing contests, where he won the hearts of spectators (including Queen Victoria, who insisted on meeting him) as well as three Waterloo Cups (the ultimate coursing trophy). All Ireland went into mourning when he died in 1871.

⬆ *Sporting icon Mick the Miller is credited with popularizing Greyhound racing, by his courage and intelligence no less than his speed.*

Marvelous Mick

A hero of the Greyhound racing track was the legendary Mick the Miller, who ran 68 races in a four-year career and was only out of the first two on five occasions. His meteoric rise from obscurity to fame made him a national hero.

After his last race in October 1931, he enjoyed a long and happy retirement, returning to the limelight in 1934 to star in the film *Wild Boy*.

Is it cricket?

Cricket is the passion of Buddy the Border Collie from Addiscombe, Surrey. Buddy taught himself to play by watching owner Andy James and his sons and has become something of a local celebrity for his sporting exploits. He catches the ball and nudges it into the stumps with his nose. His favorite position is mid-wicket, and he is just as happy playing in goal when it comes to football.

Talented tipster

One dog that preferred to attend the races as a spectator was Black Knight, socialite Pekingese of the 1940s. He was famous for his appearances (with owner Lady Munnings) at London functions from Lord Mayors' Banquets to Princess Elizabeth's wedding, and racecourses. Here he proved so talented at picking winners (barking at his choice) that Lady Munnings opened a special account for him with a bookmaker.

Boxers—or footballers

Most dogs enjoy playing ball, but only a few turn professional. However, football-playing dogs have been a popular circus act *(right)* for many years. Boxers are a favorite choice for this sport, being

A lineup of excited terriers in the starter box, waiting for the race to begin—a great way of using up surplus terrier energy!

Rough and ready

If Greyhound races are for those who take speed seriously, terrier races are for those with a sense of humor. These are usually fun events, with excited terriers pursuing a lure, sometimes over hurdles or even obstacle courses. The United States has taken the idea a step further with increasingly popular Chihuahua Races, and even Wiener Dog Races for Dachshunds.

powerful, agile, and above all, energetic. Just like human players, they can be overenthusiastic. Canine goalies at Moscow State Circus have been known to dive into a scrum for the ball, taking the goalposts with them.

Football savior

A mongrel named Pickles came to the rescue of the Football Association when the World Cup was stolen in 1966, shortly before the tournament in England. A national police investigation failed to locate the solid gold cup, and it was Pickles, out on a walk with his owner, who found it, wrapped in newspaper and dumped near a house gateway. Forty years later, his adventure inspired a 90-minute TV film.

A well-trained carriage dog adds to the elegance of the equipage. ▶▶

Pickles was awarded ▶▶ *two medals by the Italian Canine Defence League for his role in recovering the stolen World Cup.*

Elegance in motion

The most elegant of canine sports must be Carriage Dog Trials, introduced in the U.S. in the early 1900s to revive the Dalmatian's heritage as a carriage dog. No longer required to carry out their original duty of guarding coaches, the Dalmatians still run alongside or underneath carriages, or beside riders, in a sport that tests both obedience and endurance as well as the breed's natural affinity with horses.

FAITHFUL UNTO DEATH

Roman hero

2,000 years ago, a Roman dog named Delta saved the life of his master Severinus on three separate occasions, including a wolf attack. We know his story

A guard dog who died ▸▸
at Pompeii, left behind
chained to his post as his
owners fled the eruption.

because Delta died at Pompeii in A.D. 79 during the eruption of Mount Vesuvius, where the ashes preserved his body, still wearing a silver collar recording his name and his feats. In death, he lies protectively beside a child, faithful to the end.

Medieval justice

In 1361, Dragon, the hound of French knight Aubry de Montdidier, led people to the place where his murdered master lay buried. Back at court, he launched an attack on the Chevalier Macaire. This was accepted as a formal accusation of murder, and the King ordered the matter to be settled by judicial combat between man and dog. Macaire lost the duel, confessing his guilt, and Dragon saw his master avenged. His story later inspired an 18th-century theatrical melodrama.

Korean hero

Korea has had a bad press among dog-lovers because of the custom of eating dog meat, but at the same time Koreans know how to value dogs. A thousand-year-old monument records the legend of a loyal Jindo dog (Korea's best-known native breed, recognized as a National Treasure) who gave his own life to save his owner from a fire. A tree growing on the dog's grave is still venerated today as a symbol of virtue.

▲ *Many traditional Korean paintings celebrate the dog, here depicted in human costume.*

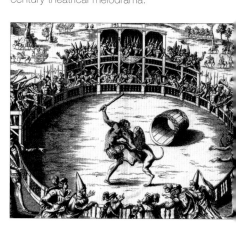

▲ *Macaire, armed with a large cudgel, battles his canine accuser in a trial by ordeal.*

Greyfriars Bobby

Bobby, a 19th-century Skye Terrier, is renowned for his devotion to his master's grave in Edinburgh Scotland. Tradition says that for 14 years Bobby

The statue of Greyfriars Bobby was sculpted from life by William Brody and has been one of the famous sights of Edinburgh since 1873.

lived in Greyfriars Kirkyard, where his master John Gray was buried. Less romantic research says he was happily rehomed after Gray's death, though he did visit his grave. His statue remains a tourist attraction to this day.

The Dog of Helvellyn

In 1805, a young man named Charles Gough became lost on Helvellyn in the English Lake District. When his body was found three months later, his favorite terrier was still guarding his master. The British public warmed to the story of the loyal "Dog of Helvellyn." Landseer painted the scene, while Wordsworth and Scott both wrote poems commemorating the dog's fidelity.

Derbyshire sheepdog

Another dog whose loyalty to her dead master earned attention was Tip the sheepdog. To this day a monument in Derbyshire, England, commemorates Tip, "who stayed by the body of her dead master, M. Joseph Tagg, on the Howden Moor for 15 weeks from December 12, 1953 to March 27, 1954."

Civil War hound

Lieutenant Louis Pfieff of the 3rd Illinois Infantry was one of thousands of soldiers who died in the 1862 Battle of Shiloh during the American Civil War. Finding his body among so many seemed an impossible task for his widow, until she found her husband's dog on the burial field. He led her to an unmarked grave, which she later learned he had guarded for 12 days, and which proved indeed to house her husband's remains.

Hachiko

Hachiko, a Japanese Akita, accompanied his master Professor Ueno to Tokyo's railroad station each morning, and each evening made his own way there to get him. In 1925, the Professor died at work and Hachiko waited at the station in vain. For the next ten days he went every evening to meet his master's train. His loyalty became famous, and his statue at the station remains a famous Tokyo landmark.

Hachiko's statue is garlanded with flowers at ⬆ the annual festival honoring his memory.

HOW WE

SEE DOGS

DOGS IN HERALDRY

The heraldic dog

Dogs have always been popular subjects in coats of arms, signifying a range of qualities—loyalty, strength, courage, vigilance, and, of course, doggedness. They come in various shapes, colors, and poses, as recognizable canines or mythical variations. In early days, breeds were limited to "noble" hounds or mastiffs, but modern coats of arms may feature anything from Labradors to Poodles.

Honorable hound

An extinct medieval hound, claimed as an ancestor by both Foxhounds and Bloodhounds, the Talbot was a favorite in heraldry. Said to have been brought to England by William the Conqueror, it was named for its association with the Talbot family, Earls of Shrewsbury. Although

⚹ *The Talbot Hound is generally described as a white dog, although heraldic Talbots come in every hue from blue to spotted.*

their former home of Alton Towers is now an amusement park, their great stone hounds still guard its entrance.

⚹ *Two Greyhounds serve as supporters on the coat of arms of the Hunter-Weston family.*

Noble Greyhound

In the Middle Ages, Greyhounds were the dogs of the nobility, which is reflected in heraldry; in France alone, more than 400 noble families feature Greyhounds on their arms. Henry VIII adopted this breed for his personal standard in 1513, and it remained associated with the House of York. The hounds appear in every possible heraldic posture, and one family, the Benwells, even boasted a winged Greyhound.

Sleuth hound

Another hound that survives only in heraldry is the Sleuth hound, a medieval forerunner of the Bloodhound, which was employed to track down thieves by scent. An example appears, collared and leashed, in the crest of the Earl of Perth and Melfort, while a demi-Sleuth hound (only the front half) crowns the Drummond coat of arms.

The crop-eared mastiff of the ▶▶ Saint-Malo coat of arms is depicted rampant—rearing up on his hind legs.

City dogs

Legend has it that Amsterdam grew up around a chapel built by Wolfert, a fisherman, and the Viking he saved from drowning. The Great Seal of Amsterdam depicts Wolfert's ship, complete with his companion, a little Spitz dog, peering over the side. Less romantically, the seal of Saint-Malo, France, features a crop-eared mastiff representing the fierce guard dogs that patrolled the city every night until 1772.

Seadogs

The seadog, a beast found only in heraldry, is best described as a distinctly fishy hound! This is a dog covered in scales, with webbed feet, a decorative scalloped fin down its back, and a broad, beaverlike tail. Colors vary; two black seadogs

◀◀ *The seadog is barely canine at all, with scales, scalloped dorsal fin, and beaver's tail.*

with golden scales support the arms of Baron Stourton, while the crest of Sir H. Delves Broughton features a red seadog's head with silver ears and fin.

Canting arms

Dogs sometimes feature in coats of arms as "canting elements" or visual puns. Thus, the arms of Hunzenschwil, in Switzerland, feature a stylish hound punning on the syllable *hund* ("hound"), and in the Middle Ages Nicholas de Kennet boasted three dogs on his shield, a kennet being a type of dog.

Modern breeds

Some modern coats of arms feature dog breeds of today. In 1909, Sir Ernest Cassel chose a Swedish Elkhound for his crest; others have chosen a wide range from Border Terriers to Foxhounds. The former Shire of Albert in Queensland, Australia, has a German Shepherd Dog and Border Collie as supporters to its coat of arms in allusion to early settlers from Germany and Scotland.

A handsome hound surmounts the Alington ⏶ coat of arms. Hounds were for centuries the most common heraldic canines, being thought most appropriate for a gentleman.

103

DOGS AND GODS

Friend of the gods

Ancient peoples often worshipped gods in animal form, from hares to hippos, but we find no trace of a canine god. Even the famous "dog-headed" Anubis of Egypt is more accurately described as a jackal. The dog's role in ancient religion is generally as guardian of the gates of the Otherworld, or simply as friend and companion of the gods; it seems our ancestors viewed the dog as too close to us to be a deity.

⬆ *Anubis in jackal form, resembling the elegant sighthounds painted in Egyptian tombs.*

Creator's companion

In a Native American myth from California, the dog exists before all other creation. The god Nagaicho takes his dog with him when he sets out to create the world and all its inhabitants. As he works he chats to his dog like any other craftsman, and when all is done, the god and his dog walk together through the new-made world. "We made it good, my dog," Nagaicho concludes, and he goes home with his dog.

Admitted to Paradise

In Muslim tradition, dogs are traditionally held to be unclean, but the dog Katmir is an exception. The legend of the Seven Sleepers of Ephesus tells how seven noble youths, walled up in a cave to die by the wicked emperor Decius in around A.D. 250, slept safely there for 309 years until it was safe to emerge.

Katmir guarded them faithfully all that time, and became one of the few animals admitted to Paradise by Mohammed.

A test of loyalty

Hindu tradition, which also considers dogs unclean, tells of the dog that faithfully accompanied King Yudhishthira on his pilgrimage to heaven. When the dog was forbidden entrance, the king refused to enter without him and turned back. The gods recalled him, for this was the last test. Had he deserted his humble companion (in fact, the god Indra in disguise), he would have shown himself unworthy to enter heaven.

Guiding the dead

Today, the Chihuahua is appreciated for its tiny size and big personality, but his ancestors were valued by the Aztecs of Mexico as guides to lead souls through the land of the dead. Funeral rites included the sacrifice of little red or yellow dogs to be interred with their masters and help them on the journey across the River of Death, for the soul might wander forever without a canine guide.

A little fat ceramic dog from Colima, Mexico, ⬆ *dated between 200 B.C. and A.D. 300, appears to represent an early Chihuahua.*

Dog star

Sirius, the brightest star in the sky, forms part of the constellation of Canis Major, "the great dog," and has been known as the Dog Star since ancient times. In Ancient Egypt, Sirius was held to be the watchdog of the River Nile: the rising of this brilliant star signaled the all-important flood season, when the Nile swelled with the tears of the goddess Isis to fertilize the farmlands.

Celestial dog

Tien'Kou, the "celestial dog" of ancient China, is a sky deity or demon associated with thunder, lightning, and meteors. He appears as a comet with a long tail of fire, and causes lunar eclipses by swallowing the moon, which he had to be forced to disgorge by people beating drums and gongs. Sometimes Tien'Kou is destructive, but at other times he helps the god Erh-lang to drive off evil spirits.

Guardian lion-dogs, or "Fo dogs," have ▼ *protected China's palaces and imperial tombs since the Han Dynasty (206 B.C.–A.D. 220).*

Buddha's little lions

The "lion dogs" of the East—China's Pekingese *(right)* and Shih Tzu, and Tibet's Lhasa Apso—were not just decorative pets, but living symbols of the lion of Buddha. When Buddhism reached China, 2,000 years ago, in the absence of real lions Buddha's lion companion became a lion dog *(above)*, and the little dogs of palace and monastery were bred to increase their resemblance to artists' impressions of the lion.

DOGS AND THE CHURCH

Unbiblical beasts

Historically, the Church never quite trusted dogs, although at the same time many individuals within the Church, from popes to humble priests, have held dogs in the highest esteem. A certain coolness toward canines stemmed from the fact that the Bible originated in a land where dogs were considered unclean, but at least the dog never fared as badly as the cat in Western religious tradition.

Tobit's dog

The one Biblical dog occurs in the apocryphal *Book of Tobit*. He belongs to Tobit's son Tobiah, and accompanies Tobiah on a journey with the angel Raphael. The charming detail that the dog showed his joy on their return to Nineveh "by fawning and wagging his tail" was added to the text in the 4th century by translator St. Jerome, clearly a man who knew dogs.

Church founder?

A dog may have been responsible for the creation of the Church of England!

Perhaps Henry VIII was forced to found the ⬆ *Church of England by a misbehaving Spaniel.*

When Henry VIII sent an ambassador to the Pope to request a divorce from his first wife, the ambassador's Spaniel bit the Pope's toe—an act unlikely to predispose him in Henry's favor. The Pope's refusal of his request led to Henry's split from the Catholic Church—did the dog's misdeed perhaps contribute to it all?

Church monuments

Dogs are common on medieval monumental brasses and tomb effigies, usually conventional emblems of fidelity, but sometimes portraits of specific family pets. At Deerhurst, Gloucestershire, the Cassey family's 14th-century memorial brass shows a little dog lying at the feet of Lady Alice Cassey and is labeled with his name, "Tirri"; the oldest known pet memorial in England.

⬆ *Tobiah's dog waits patiently while Raphael directs his master toward the city of Rages.*

Misericord mutts

Medieval woodcarvers and stonemasons filled medieval churches with a profusion of scenes from daily life or popular stories and even pagan imagery. Dog-lovers can find much to delight them in carved corbels and misericords, where dogs abound, some stylized, some evidently modeled from life, perhaps even representing the craftsman's own favorite companion.

A carving at Swaffham Church, Norfolk, ▲ depicts the pet of a peddler who found buried treasure and then paid to rebuild the church.

Dog doors

Visitors to old country churches in Wales may be surprised to see a small door cut into the bottom of a church door. This is a dog door, provided for the convenience of sheepdogs that used to attend service with their masters. It is not clear whether this was provided so that they could pop out from time to time to check their sheep, or to spare them boredom during long sermons!

Dog Chapel

The Dog Chapel at St. Johnsbury, Vermont, was opened in 1999 by folk artist Stephen Huneck as the "first dog church," to honor his five dogs, who helped him recover from a serious illness.

Carved dogs support the pews, stained-glass windows depict haloed Labradors, and a winged dog tops the steeple. Dogs are as welcome as their owners—the sign outside proclaims, "All creeds, all breeds, no dogma."

Dog Whippers

Until well into the 19th century, dogs regularly attended services with their owners. Some churches even provided a separate pew for the local squire's dogs. Most dogs knew how to behave in church, but officials known as Dog Whippers were appointed to eject unruly canines, as well as dealing with disorderly children and waking up any snoozing members of the congregation.

Worshippers and their dogs attend an Animal ▲ Service at the Church of St. Paul's, London.

DOGS AND SAINTS

Saint's friend

St. Roche, a 14th-century French healer, is said to have owed his life to a dog. He was nursing plague victims, but when he caught the plague himself no one would help him, except Roquet, the dog of a local nobleman, who brought him food each day and licked his sores until he recovered. Roquet appears in many pictures of the saint and for centuries St. Roche's feast day, August 16th, was celebrated by a Blessing of Dogs.

Dog-headed saint...

St. Christopher, patron of travelers, is the only saint with a dog's head. Tradition says Christopher was an ogre with a dog's head and cannibal habits, until he was converted to Christianity and tortured for his faith. In the fires of martyrdom, his canine head was transformed into a face "as beautiful as a new rose," though medieval paintings often portray him as the dog-headed saint.

...and dog saint

Guinefort the Greyhound was the only dog saint. French legend tells how he saved his master's baby from a snake, only to be killed by his master in the mistaken belief that he had attacked the infant. Local peasants regarded him as a saint, and took their children to his grave for healing. Although the Church learned of the cult of St. Guinefort in the 13th century and banned it, it survived into the early 20th century.

Guide dog

St. Margaret of Cortona (1247–1297), a beautiful Italian peasant girl, was a nobleman's mistress, until one day his dog returned home alone and led her to

An angel tends St. Roche's sores while Roquet the hound looks on, as depicted in the early 16th-century Prayerbook of the Abbess of Messines.

St. Margaret of Cortona, with attendant hound seated at her feet.

DOG BIZ

Monks of the Hospice of St. Bernard in 1923, with more athletic dogs than the modern breed.

his master's murdered body. Shocked into penitence, Margaret entered a convent and was eventually canonized. The dog that led her to her conversion is portrayed with her in art, sitting at her feet or tugging urgently at the hem of her robe.

Mad dogs' patron

Little is known of St. Blaise, who was probably an Armenian bishop of the early 4th century. He is patron saint of woolcombers and, more obscurely, of mad dogs. Legend says that when St. Peter was handing out responsibilities to various saints, he invited Blaise to become patron saint of young girls. The horrified saint said he would rather look after mad dogs, so St. Peter took him at his word!

St. Bernard

The saint most irrevocably linked with dogs today is St. Bernard, though he had no association with them until seven centuries after his death! However, he did found St. Bernard's Hospice as a resthouse for travelers through the Alps, where later the monks trained their dogs to rescue lost travelers and eventually evolved the breed that became the famous St. Bernard dog of today.

Hunters' hounds

St. Hubert, an 8th-century French bishop, is credited with developing the great tracking dogs of the Middle Ages known as St. Hubert's Hounds, the probable ancestors of our Bloodhounds. Legend says he turned from hunting to God after his

St. Hubert's dogs, having led him toward his sign from God, wait respectfully as he kneels before the sacred hart (stag).

hounds followed a holy white hart (stag) bearing a crucifix. In France, Belgium, and Ireland St. Hubert's feast day (November 3rd) is still marked by a Blessing of the Hounds.

DOGS IN LEGEND

Cerberus

In Greek mythology, Cerberus, the three-headed watchdog, guards the gate of Hades, the world of the dead, allowing no living soul to enter nor any of the dead to escape. Various heroes tackled him from time to time. Hercules had to overcome the great hound as his twelfth labor and bring him into the land of the living, while the minstrel Orpheus, seeking his lost wife in Hades, lulled the watchdog asleep with his music.

⬆ *Three-headed Cerberus continues to capture the imagination, as depicted here by visionary poet-painter William Blake (1757–1827).*

Actaeon's hounds

Greek myth also tells of the hunter Actaeon, who accidentally came upon the goddess Diana bathing in a pool and was turned into a stag by the irate goddess, to be torn apart by his own hounds. For dog-lovers, the high point of the story is that we are told the names of all 48 hounds, from Asbolos ("sooty") to Laelaps ("hurricane"), names that were perpetuated for many years in English hunting packs.

Garm

Garm is the Vikings' version of Cerberus, a monstrous four-eyed hound that guards the entrance to Helheim, Norse realm of the dead. Anyone who had given food to the poor in their life could appease Garm with Hel-cake; the less generous were in trouble. At Ragnarok, the Norse Doomsday when the world ends, Garm will ally with the giants in their battle against the gods, when he and the war god Tyr will kill each other.

The Wild Hunt

Celtic legends tell of a huntsman who rides the night sky with his hounds in pursuit of unearthly quarry—the lord of the underworld hunting, or King Arthur, or wicked Cornish Squire Dando paying for his sins. His hounds are known as the Cwn Annwn (Hounds of Hell), Gabriel Ratchet, Wish Hounds, or Yeth Hounds, though unromantic scientists say they originated in the houndlike cry of wild geese flying through the night.

Luigi Vanvitelli's dramatic fountain at the ▶▶ *Palazzo Reale (1774), Caserta, Campania portrays the death of Actaeon.*

⬆ *Marvelously convoluted hounds with inter-twined serpentine bodies are a frequently occurring theme in Celtic knotwork.*

The hound of Culann

In Irish mythology, the hero Cuchulainn ("hound of Culann") earns his name when, still a child, in self-defense he kills the mighty guard dog of Culann the smith, and in apology to Culann offers to acts as his hound until a canine replacement can be trained. Later, as the great champion of the Red Branch of warriors protecting Ulster, Cuchulainn becomes the guardian of the kingdom—the Hound of Ulster.

Fairy hounds

The fairy hounds of British folklore are white with red ears (which may explain why the Celts valued white-and-red dogs, giving us the Welsh Springer Spaniel and Irish Red and White Setter. In Wiltshire, they say that such a hound haunts the Stone Age burial chamber known as the Devil's Den, so avoid the site at midnight—seeing the fairy hounds brings misfortune on mortals.

The Cu Sith

Another Celtic myth features the Cu Sith, the fairy dog of the Scottish Highlands that roams the moors seeking to carry off mortal women to the Otherworld to serve as wet-nurses for fairy babies. He is the size of a bull, with a long braided tail, and his dark green color makes him unique among mythical canines.

King Arthur's dog

Early Welsh writers credit the legendary King Arthur with the possession of a hound, Caball, hero of two epic boar hunts and said to have left his paw print on a Welsh mountain. Sadly, Arthur's dog originated in a mistake. An early scribe, tired or careless, misread Latin *caballus* "horse" as a name and decided it must apply to a hound belonging to the king—and a new member of the Arthurian world was born.

⬆ *The spirit of Culainn appears to his mother, from* The Songs of Ossian *as depicted by Danish artist N.A. Abildgaard (1743–1809).*

BLACK PHANTOMS

A national institution

All over the British Isles, legends tell of a phantom black dog that haunts wild regions. Huge, shaggy, and fiery-eyed, he has many names—Old or Black Shuck, Galleytrot, Padfoot, Barguest, Trash, Skryker, etc.—and is usually seen as a portent of evil but sometimes as a guardian spirit. Today, few believe in the Black Dog; but he may live on in the mysterious "black panthers" reported in the British countryside.

The Black Dog of Bouley Bay is featured on a Jersey stamp, and also has a tavern named after him.

Beast at Bungay

Suffolk boasts the most dramatic Black Dog encounter. On August 4th, 1577, a fiery black dog burst into Bungay Church during the service, killing two people and injuring another, repeating his performance at nearby Blythburgh, where he killed two more and sent the church spire crashing through the roof. As he rampaged out of the church, he left deep scorch marks on the door, still visible today.

◀◀ *The blackened claw marks of the Black Dog of Bungay are still to be seen on the door of Blythburgh Church in Suffolk.*

Beast at Bouley

In Jersey in the Channel Islands, legend tells of the Black Dog of Bouley Bay, which roamed by night terrorizing locals with its burning eyes and the sound of its dragging chain. It never attacked directly, but circled its victims at great speed until they were cowering in fear. The legend was perpetuated by smugglers to discourage people from going out at night and catching them in the act.

Warwick haunting

Legend says that a black dog once haunted Warwick Castle. The tale goes that a local woman, Moll Bloxham, earned her living selling stolen supplies from the castle until the Earl of Warwick caught her. She took her revenge after her death by haunting the castle in the form of a

⬆ *Warwick Castle, no longer haunted by a Black Dog, is now a popular tourist attraction.*

huge black dog, but exorcists managed to drive the dog from the castle tower into the river below, and it was never seen again.

Man's best friend became ▶▶ something more sinister to people walking home at night, before streetlights became common.

Spiritual black dog

"The black dog is on his back" is an old and graphic term to describe someone suffering from depression—what Robert Louis Stephenson called a "terrifying nursery metaphor." Samuel Johnson and Sir Winston Churchill both knew their bouts of melancholy as "the black dog"; more recently, in 2002, an Australian medical foundation dealing with mood disorders including depression was named the Black Dog Institute.

Friendly phantoms

Not all Black Dogs are sinister. In many accounts, the only frightening thing about them is the way they appear out of nowhere and disappear just as mysteriously. In some parts of England, they are even helpful, taking on the role of

guardians of travelers on lonely roads, when they may ward off attackers or simply provide company, vanishing when their protégé reaches home.

Literary black dog

The most famous literary descendant of the tradition is surely the title character of Conan Doyle's 1902 novel, *The Hound of the Baskervilles*, in which deaths on Dartmoor are blamed on just such a supernatural dog. Although Sherlock Holmes proves that the beast is no phantom but merely an instrument of the villain, the image of the giant hound continues to scare readers and inspire film directors.

Black Dogs Worldwide

In El Salvador, the fearful black Cadejo pursues night travelers; in Catalan legend, Dip, a Satanic black dog, sucks people's blood. An American example is the Black Dog of Hanging Hills, Connecticut—see it three times, and you die—while Australia has a ghostly Black Dog guarding Picton churchyard, New South Wales, which has been known to chase visitors out of the graveyard.

◀◀ *Phantom black dogs may be ghost dogs, human ghosts in canine form, or the hounds of hell.*

DOG SUPERSTITIONS

Dogs aren't scary

Considering the prevalence of dogs in human societies, there are surprisingly few canine superstitions. In general, animal superstitions focus on beasts associated with goddess worship (and therefore are linked with fears of witchcraft), from cats to crows. The dog, "Man's Best Friend," does not fall into this group and generally inspires trust rather than fear; hence the dearth of doggy superstitions.

Howling dogs

The haunting sound of a dog's howl, on the other hand, is often considered an ill omen. A dog howling outside your house at night signifies bad luck, as does a dog howling at an open door, while a dog howling three times at night, then falling silent means a death nearby. If someone in the house is ill, a dog howling at night is a bad omen, but it can be reversed by reaching under the bed and turning over a shoe.

In sickness and in health

A traditional cure for illness was to sleep with the family dog, hoping the illness would transfer to the animal. Similarly, to cure a cough, people would take a hair from the patient's head, put it between two slices of buttered bread and feed it to a dog, saying, "Eat well, you hound, may you be sick and I be sound." A bite from a mad dog was treated by feeding the victim some of the dog's hairs, or a piece of its cooked liver.

Canine behavior

Omens have been seen in various things dogs do. A dog digging a big hole in your garden is said to be digging a grave, a sign of a forthcoming death in the family. A strange dog coming to the house means you can expect a new friendship, but meeting a barking dog first thing in the morning means bad luck. In India, a dog sniffing your left limbs signifies riches, but if it sniffs your right limbs, danger is coming.

Dreams

Dream about a dog, you will have great gains and constant friends.

Dream that a dog bites you, your best friend will become your worst enemy.

Dream of dogs fighting (above right), you will need to settle an argument between friends. Dream that you hear barking dogs, expect bad news and difficulties.

Dream that a dog is barking at you, you will have plenty of friends.

Dream of a large, friendly dog, you have a powerful protector.

Dream of a mad dog, strangers will attack you (but if you kill the dog, all will be well, and if

good omen, meeting a spotted dog on your way to a business appointment signifies that your business will go well, and a dog with a white spot on its forehead also brings good luck.

Wedding ritual

In 2003, a nine-year-old girl in eastern India was married to a stray dog as part of a ritual to ward off an "evil spell" on her. More than a hundred guests attended the wedding. It was a happy wedding: for little Karnamoni as it meant freedom from fear (with the assurance that she could take a human husband later), and for Bacchan the dog it provided a home where he would no longer have to scavenge for scraps —a happy ending for both!

someone else kills it, you will have a staunch protector).

Dream of a black dog, beware negative aspects of your life.

Dream of a white dog, cultivate the spiritual side of your life.

Dream of a sleeping dog, you are unaware of something important.

Colors

Black dogs, like many other black animals, are sometimes considered unlucky, and, in particular, being followed persistently by a black dog is a bad omen. However, seeing a white dog before noon, or three white dogs together, is a

⬆ *A bronze plaque on the Charles Bridge in Prague depicts King Wenceslas IV of Bohemia and St. John of Nepomuk, whom the king killed for refusing to betray the queen's secrets that had been told to him in confession. A local superstition holds that touching the king's dog will bring good luck and many hands have polished it to a bright sheen.*

A white spot, or thumb- ▶▶ print, on a dog's forehead brings good luck.

GHOST DOGS

The Mauthe Dog

Peel Castle on the Isle of Man, Great Britain, was long famous for its spectral black dog, the Moddey Dhoo or Mauthe Dog, which haunted the guard room. The guards treated him with respect—wisely, since a drunken guard who failed to do so never spoke again, and died three days later. The ghost dog is said to have been the pet of 13th-century Bishop Simon, whose grave, uncovered in 1871, was shared by a dog buried at his feet.

Paws in the night

When the owner of Ballechin House, Scotland, lay dying in 1874, he unnerved his family by insisting that he would return in the body of his favorite spaniel. Upon his death, they shot the spaniel, along with his other 13 dogs. For the next 20 years, until it was exorcised, the house was the scene of sinister hauntings, notably the disembodied paws of a black dog traversing the rooms.

▲ *Noltland Castle, Scotland, home of the ghostly Boky Hound, is only one of several sites in the Orkneys haunted by phantom dogs.*

lurks under the castle staircase. Legend says 13th-century knight Sir David Balfour killed his dog when it knocked his drink over, only to find the beast had saved his life—the drink had been poisoned by his faithless wife. The dog's ghost has haunted the castle ever since, heralding the death of Balfour family members with bloodcurdling howls.

Countess's comforter

Restoration work at the Jacobean manor of Ham House, southwest London, uncovered the grave of a small dog in the orangery. Perhaps this explains the many sightings by visitors of the ghost of a King Charles Spaniel scampering around the house. The ghost dog is said to resemble the spaniel that appears in paintings of the Countess of Dysart, who lived there in the 17th century.

Castle specter

Noltland Castle, in the Orkney Islands of Scotand, is haunted by the Boky Hound, which

Blue guardian

The Rose Hill Blue Dog is one of Maryland's best-known ghosts. The story goes that he guards the buried gold of his master, a peddler who was killed by thieves in the late 18th century on Rose Hill Road, outside Port Tobacco. Sightings of the Blue Dog have been reported by many witnesses, including President George Washington, and residents claim to hear him howling on cold winter nights.

Faithful Newfoundland

In 1861, Captain John McNeill Boyd lost his life trying to save the crew of a wrecked ship. His faithful Newfoundland dog accompanied his funeral procession, then pined to death lying on his grave in Glasnevin Cemetery, Dublin, Ireland. Its ghost has been seen many times, both at his grave and also sitting by his memorial statue in Dublin Cathedral.

An photograph of a tea party at Tingewick, Buckinghamshire, England, in 1916 captured the image of an unseen "headless ghost dog."

Tennessee ghost

A canine ghost known as "Long Dog" roams the highway near Surgoinsville, Tennessee. The story goes that he died in the 1820s, trying to protect his owners from a murderous attack by a local outlaw. Thereafter, his ghost was seen running alongside wagons and even jumping aboard, apparently seeking his long-lost family. Occasional sightings are still reported today, although faster traffic seems to have discouraged him.

In folklore, phantom dogs are sometimes seen as witches' familiars, for a prevalent belief held that the Devil might appear in the form of a black dog. Here the sorceress Guillemette Babin is portrayed riding just such a monstrous black dog through the night.

Ghostly Great Dane

Los Angeles Pet Cemetery is the last resting-place of the pets of many of the rich and famous, and sightings of several animal ghosts have been reported there. Most conspicuous is Rudolph Valentino's Great Dane, Kabar, buried there in 1929. A particularly friendly ghost, Kabar makes frequent appearances, and many visitors to his grave report being licked by the spectral dog.

FAIRY STORIES AND FABLES

Dog in a manger

Aesop told a fable of a dog that was lying in a manger on the hay *(above)*. When the cattle came in to eat the hay, he drove them off with snaps and snarls. "What a selfish beast!" one of the cows commented. "He can't eat himself, yet he won't let those eat who can." The moral: People often begrudge others what they can't enjoy themselves.

Luxury versus liberty

Another Aesop fable tells how a hungry wolf encountered a well-fed dog and asked him how he found all his food. The dog said that his master fed him. Then the wolf asked why the dog had a bare spot on his neck, and the dog explained that his master had put an iron collar on him, which chafed. "You can keep your luxury," the wolf told him. "I don't fancy it, if it means a sore neck from an iron chain!"

Chasing wolves

Aesop also told of a dog that was very pleased with himself as he chased a wolf away, imagining that the wolf was fleeing for fear of his strength and speed. But at a safe distance from the farm, the wolf stopped and said, "Don't imagine I'm running away from you! I'm just afraid of being chased down by your master." The moral: Don't credit yourself with good qualities that are actually someone else's.

Big eyes and little dogs

In European fairy stories, dogs tend to play "bit parts" rather than major roles. There are the three dogs with "eyes as big as saucers," "eyes as big as platters," and "eyes as big as millstones" who guard the witch's treasure in Hans Christian Anderson's *The Tinderbox*. At the other extreme, in several quest tales the hero is sent to find a tiny dog, and a magical helper brings him a dog so small it fits into a nutshell.

Beauty and the dog

An English version of "Beauty and the Beast" has a dog playing the role of the Beast. A huge dog saves the life of a merchant and

▲ *When the well-dressed dog and the shabby wolf compare lifestyles, the wolf prefers his freedom.*

In Hans Christian Anderson's sad tale of The Snowman, *the snowman achieves his wish to go indoors, where he melts in the heat, and the yard dog, a former pet now banished and chained outside, can never go indoors again.*

demands his daughter as a reward. He keeps the merchant's daughter at his home until she stops calling him "a great, foul, small-tooth dog" and christens him "Sweet-as-a-Honeycomb." This breaks the spell, turning him into a handsome young man, and they marry and live happily ever after.

The lost fairy dog

In a Welsh folktale, a woman rescues a lost fairy dog and cares for it. When the fairies come for it, they ask whether she would rather have her cowyard clean or dirty. She gives the right answer (dirty—a clean cowyard means a shortage of cows!) and is rewarded, her herd being doubled. Her foolish cousin mistreats a fairy dog, answers the riddle incorrectly, and is suitably punished.

The dog hat

A Chinese folktale tells of a rich merchant and his wife, whose long-awaited baby was stolen by their wicked sister-in-law. Their brown dog saved the day, retrieving the baby and restoring him to his family. The happy mother named her child "Dog Son" and made him a hat depicting a dog's face to honor the faithful hound. To this day, "dog hats" are still worn by children in southeast China.

Musicians of Bremen

A fairy tale recorded by the Brothers Grimm tells how a donkey, a rooster, a dog, and a cat head to the town of Bremen to escape from their cruel masters. En route, they accidentally frighten robbers away from a house when they stand on each other's backs and sing to beg for food. They move into the cottage, scaring off the robbers when they try to move back in again, and live there happily ever after.

The story of The Musicians of Bremen *is commemorated by a 6.6-foot (2-m) high bronze statue erected in 1951 near the city hall.*

DOGS IN LITERATURE

In the beginning

The earliest fictional dog on record is Argos, loyal hound of the hero Odysseus in the Greek epic, *The Odyssey*. During Odysseus's ten years' absence from his island home of Ithaca,

Argos has grown old and neglected, yet he is the only creature to recognize his master upon his return. Having waited faithfully for that moment, he is now too feeble to do more than wag his tail and die, a commentary on less loyal humans.

⬆ *More faithful than any human, the aged Argos is the first member of Odysseus' household to recognize his master.*

Thy Servant a Dog

Rudyard Kipling wrote with affection of many dogs. In *Thy Servant a Dog* (1930) he wrote from the point of view of Boots, a Scottish Terrier, using childlike language that some today find cutesy, while others recognize in it their own dogs' approach to life. Boots recounts the small adventures of life with his family, his companion Slippers, his enemy Kitchen Cat, and his friend Ravager the Foxhound.

The silent hound

The only canine hero in medieval romance is Husdent, the noble hound of the tragic lovers Tristan and Isolde. Accompanying the lovers into exile, he has to learn to hunt without

The lovers Tristan and Isolde, depicted in ▸▸ *stained glass by William Morris (1834–1896), are attended in death by watchful hounds.*

baying, in order not to betray their hiding place. When they part, he is Isolde's comforter; later, when Tristan reappears, so ravaged by grief that even Isolde fails to recognize him, faithful Husdent knows his master at once.

Patrasche

A Dog of Flanders (1872), by Ouida, is a Dickensian tale of poverty, in which orphaned Nello has no chance to become the artist he longs to be. His chief comfort is the dog Patrasche who supports Nello and his grandfather by pulling a milk cart, before, after many hard times, boy and dog die of cold together outside Antwerp Cathedral. The story has been filmed at least five times, and Antwerp now boasts a statue of Patrasche.

Poor Bull's-eye

In Charles Dickens' *Oliver Twist* (1838), the brutish dog Bull's-eye serves to highlight the villainy of his equally brutish master Bill Sikes.

Horror hound

Representing the genre of horror fiction is Stephen King's 1981 novel, *Cujo*, in which rabies transforms Cujo, a St. Bernard, from man's best friend into man's worst nightmare. Most of the novel focuses on the ordeal of local housewife Donna Trenton, trapped in her car with her four-year-old son for three days while Cujo rampages outside. A 1983 film version had problems persuading its St. Bernard star to act sufficiently fierce!

A difficult dog

American humorist James Thurber wrote of (and drew) many of the dogs in his life, from Rex the Bull Terrier, who carried home a chest of drawers just for the challenge, to Muggs the Airedale *(below)*, "the dog that bit people." Thurber gives a hilarious account of life with the irascible Muggs, a dog loved only by Thurber's mother, who sent boxes of candy every Christmas to the people he bit—40 or more of them.

⬆ *Bull's-eye the dog is an inseparable part of our image of the villainous Bill Sikes.*

Repaying ill-treatment with canine loyalty, he shares his master's fate, leaping to his death as Sikes falls from the rooftops. Dickens describes Bull's-eye as "a white, shaggy dog" but on stage and screen he is always portrayed as a Bull Terrier, usually a Stafford.

CHILDREN'S STORIES

A lot of spots

Few dog stories have as many canine characters as Dodie Smith's famous 1956 novel *The Hundred and One Dalmatians*. The story was inspired by the author's own beloved Dalmatians—and a casual comment from a friend that the first of the tribe, Pongo "would make a nice fur coat." The birth of 15 puppies to Smith's dogs Buzz and Folly, and the resuscitation of the runt of the litter, also made their way into the novel.

⬆ *Nana the canine nursemaid in* Peter Pan, *seen here giving a ride to one of her charges, is traditionally played by a human actor.*

⬆ *Walt Disney's animated film of* One Hundred and One Dalmatians, *released in 1961, was one of the studio's most popular films.*

Nursemaid Nana

Real-life dogs also inspired the creation of Nana, the canine nursemaid in J.M. Barrie's *Peter Pan* (1904), whose responsible attitude toward the children she tends contrasts with their father's immaturity. Nana was a combination of Barrie's St. Bernard, Porthos, and his successor Luath, a Newfoundland. For the first stage production, Arthur Lupino, playing Nana, based his role on a study of Luath's real-life behavior.

Afghan mischief

Frank Muir's series of children's books about an accident-prone Afghan Hound puppy started with *What-a-Mess* in 1977 and continued with ten more titles and a TV series. Illustrator Joseph Wright depicts the well-meaning hero What-a-Mess (officially Prince Amir of Kinjan, but known by the cry his adventures always elicit) as endearingly scruffy and bearing no resemblance to the aloof Afghans of the show ring.

⬆ *Connal the dog played the part of Timmy in the TV dramatization of* The Famous Five.

Famous fifth

The "Famous Five" of Enid Blyton's well-known series (21 books, written between 1942 and 1963) comprise four children and the dog Timmy. Originally found as a stray by tomboy George, Timmy is the idealized child's dog, intelligent, obedient (apart from a tendency to chase rabbits) and protective, and plays a major part in all the gang's adventures.

Magic Dougal

The children's animated TV series *The Magic Roundabout* was a 1960s icon that retains its place in the affections of children and adults

⬆ *Dougal's grumpy character in the English version was based on Tony Hancock.*

alike. Created in France by Serge Danot in 1965, but given an extra dimension by Eric Thompson's English dialogue, its cast included the unforgettable shaggy dog Dougal, with a grumpy personality inspired by comedian Tony Hancock and an insatiable appetite for sugar lumps.

Not in Kansas anymore

Everyone knows Toto, Dorothy's little dog in Frank Baum's *The Wizard of Oz* (1907), and most of us at once envisage the classic 1939 movie version with Judy Garland and her Cairn Terrier *(right)*. But Toto was not always a Cairn. Illustrator W. Denslow made him a Cairn for the first book in the Oz series, but later

books were illustrated by R. Neill, who portrayed him as a French Bulldog, perhaps in honor of Quinn, his own Frenchie.

Wags on wheels

A crippled Chihuahua abandoned on a California street seems an unlikely hero, but "Wheely Willy" is now famous worldwide. Willy's indomitable spirit and joy in life as he raced around his "canine wheelchair" made him an inspiring hospital visitor for paralyzed patients. His story, *How Willy Got His Wheels*, by Deborah Turner and Diana Mohler, led him to stardom and won the 1998 Maxwell Award for Children's Literature.

MOVIE MUTTS

It began with Blair

The first canine film star was Blair, a Collie owned by British film director Cecil Hepworth. In 1905, Hepworth made a six-minute film, *Rescued by Rover*, in which Blair starred as a dog that saves his master's baby from kidnappers. The film was such a success that the negatives fell apart and Hepworth had to re-shoot it twice! Blair starred in four sequels before his death in 1910.

Rin Tin Tin

Found as a bombed-out refugee in war-torn France and adopted by an American soldier, the German Shepherd Rin Tin Tin grew up to become one of Hollywood's favorite stars of the 1920s, receiving some 10,000 fan letters a week. The 26 silent films he made for Warner Brothers saved the studio from financial ruin and earned him the nickname of "the mortgage lifter."

▲ *Dog star Rin Tin Tin was aptly honored with a star on the Hollywood Walk of Fame.*

Lassie Come Home

The movies' best-known canine is heroic Collie Lassie, whose saga began in 1943 with *Lassie Come Home* and continues to this day. The first dog star to play the role was Pal, a Collie whose first owner rejected him as untrainable! The 2006 remake was the first not to use a direct Pal descendant, as none was available with a pet passport for international travel.

In Beethoven's ▶▶ *2nd (1993), the lovable St. Bernard was played by two dogs, a man in a dog costume, and an articulated head for close-up facial expressions.*

Beethoven

Beethoven (1992), a box office hit about a lovable but accident-prone St. Bernard, was followed by a series of sequels all the way up to *Beethoven's 5th* (2003). Although the films didn't pull any punches about the problems of living with a lumbering large dog given to drooling, the dog-buying public was enchanted—and breed rescue groups found themselves inundated with young St. Bernards that had outgrown their welcome.

Mandy

Nobody thought a Pekingese could be trained for film work until Sinodun Su Mandy Tu hit the screen in the 1960s. Mandy loved the spotlight, enjoying special effects "bombing" in *The Yellow Rolls Royce* (1964) and pulling a miniature troika in *Diamonds for Breakfast* (1968). She also appeared in many commercials and TV series, and even the London Harness Horse Parade, where she carried a rabbit passenger in her troika.

MORE TO WATCH	
Old Yeller (1957)	Spike, from the same trainer as the Lassie collies, was initially rejected by Disney for the role of Old Yeller because he was too friendly. It took weeks to teach him to act tough!
Turner and Hooch (1989)	The film that made Dogues de Bordeaux a fashionable breed. Canine star Hooch was played by 11-year-old Beasley.
K-9 (1989)	Sniffer dog Koton was played by Jerry Lee, a real-life police dog that returned to work after filming and was killed on duty in 1991 apprehending a criminal.
White Fang (1991)	Jed, a handsome wolf-dog hybrid, played White Fang. He also played a wolf in both *The Thing* (1982) and *The Journey of Natty Gann* (1985).
As Good as It Gets (1997)	Scene-stealing Brussels Griffon Verdell was played by a team of dogs, most notably Jill, described as "really the fourth lead in the picture." The film was nearly called *A Dog's Story*.
Because of Winn-Dixie (2005)	Scruffy mutt Winn-Dixie is played by Scott and Laiko, Picardy Shepherds that had to be imported from France as the breed is so rare in the U.S., and then given a crash course in acting.

Frank the Pug

Sci-fi comedy *Men in Black* (1997) introduced Frank the Pug, a wisecracking alien who only looks like a Pug dog. Rescue dog Mushu was such a hit that his role was expanded in the 2002 sequel (by which time, aged seven, he needed a touch of mascara to cover graying whiskers). As Frank, he wore a $9,000 Italian suit, and his natural acting ability was supplemented by computer animation enabling him to talk and even sing.

Benji

Benji (1974) was the first "doggy" film to bring a mongrel into the spotlight, and its star, the appealing Higgins, became an instant hit. The film's success led to a run of Benji movies, with Higgins' daughter taking over the role when he grew too old. The current Benji, fourth of that name, was rescued from an animal shelter to carry on the tradition.

Lovable mutt Benji helped to popularize shaggy ⬆ *mongrels, unlike traditional pedigree dog stars.*

CANINE ACTORS AND STUNT DOGS

Working in the movies

Many canine film stars are trained by professionals, but others are well-trained pets whose owners sign on with agencies. To make a career out of film work, dogs need good looks, a good temperament, and loads of personality. They also need to be trained to at least basic level, to be able to ignore distractions when working and ideally to follow hand signals at a distance.

▲ Famous actor Pippin, trained by Ann Head, takes her turn on the other side of the camera.

Step by step

Handlers train dogs to carry out amazingly elaborate scenes by breaking these down into sequences. For example, top trainer Ann Head explained how she taught a dog to "play chess" with a string of commands put together. A mere five instructions had the dog positioned at the chess table, picking up a chess piece and moving it slowly across the table, then placing it on the required square.

Classic actors

Great canine actors don't just obey commands, they also portray emotions convincingly. Strongheart, a German Shepherd star of the 1920s, brought tears to audiences' eyes in *The Silent Call* when he fell to the ground and "wept" at the loss of his mate and puppies. Forty years later another German Shepherd, Radar, had the same astounding ability to recognize the atmosphere of a scene and act accordingly.

⩲ *Clever editing can make a game look like a convincing fight.*

Ferocious fights

How do you teach a dog to fake a convincing fight? You don't need to. Movie dogfights are achieved by filming hours of play and using edited highlights. Wounds are painted on, and growls dubbed in later. In *White Fang*, the hero wore a fur collar made to match his own coat during his "fight" with the Pit Bull, who chewed on this "fake neck" while the two dogs, actually close friends, enjoyed a play-fight.

A dangerous jump

Beethoven includes a scene in which two puppies escape from thieves by jumping out of a moving van. The stunt was planned so that the dogs ran no risk. The van moved very slowly while they jumped only as far as a platform attached to the back. Separate shots of paws hitting the ground were taken when the trainer dropped the puppies gently from waist-height. Trick camera angles and clever editing made their leap look real.

Dogs can be trained to perform impressive stunts. Here a member of the Pathfinders Dog Display Team soars through a blazing hoop with complete confidence.

⋏ *Fly the sheepdog and Babe the pig in an uncharacteristically quiet moment of the film.*

Tricks with technology

Films like *Babe*, the story of a piglet raised by a sheepdog, can achieve astonishing effects with modern technology, but even though *Babe* was enhanced with animatronics and digital computer animation, 80 percent of the action was performed by live animals. It took 64 trainers, 970 animals, and three years to achieve that result, and even Fly the motherly sheepdog required nine dogs to play her role.

Vampire hounds

The vampire movie *Blade: Trinity* includes a scene when three vampire dogs—two Rottweilers and a Pomeranian—pursue the hero, crashing through a window and falling to the ground several stories below. The dogs were "vampirized" by computer graphics to exaggerate their mouths, while the impressive-looking leap was in reality through harmless break-away glass to a padded floor just below.

CARTOON CANINES

Snowy

Belgian cartoonist Hergé (Georges Remi) invented Tintin the boy detective back in 1929. Since then, Tintin and his devoted white Fox Terrier companion have become world-famous, with their adventures translated into more than 50 languages. Originally named Milou (after Hergé's girlfriend Marie-Louise), the little dog is better known in the English translation as Snowy.

⏶ *Tintin's constant companion, Snowy the Fox Terrier, in a scene from the animated film,* Tintin and the Lake of Sharks *(1972).*

Boot

Maurice Dodd's strip *The Perishers* (1957 to date) has been described as a working-class British version of America's *Peanuts*. Instead of Snoopy, it has Boot, a big scruffy dog who gradually evolved into an Old English Sheepdog, inspiring Dodd to buy one of his own, Bob. Bob's seaside explorations led to the saga of the Boot's annual encounters with a clan of argumentative pool-dwelling crabs that know him only as the "Eyeballs-in-the-Sky."

Pluto

Pluto *(above)*, hero (and bit-part player) of more than a hundred Disney cartoons, is best known as Mickey Mouse's pet dog, though he took up this role only in his third cartoon (*The Moose Hunt*, 1931), having first appeared in *The Chain Gang* (1930). Described as a Bloodhound, he is more doglike than most Disney cartoon canines, which may account for his enduring appeal. Despite his age, he is still featured in new animations.

Fred Basset

Alex Graham's creation, Fred the Basset Hound, has kept his place in the public's affections since his first appearance in 1963, surviving Graham's death in 1991 with reruns continuing to this day. Unlike other canine cartoon heroes, he leads a quiet life with his human family and doggy friends such as Jock the terrier, the gentle humor arising from the natural encounters of a dog's life.

Marmaduke

Brad Anderson's comic strip about the Winslow family and their Great Dane, Marmaduke, made its debut in 1954 and today is syndicated in more than 20 countries. Originally inspired by his parents' Boxer, Bruno, the strip focuses on the gentle humor in the relationship between the dog and his humans. Marmaduke is one of the few cartoon dogs that do not talk or think in word balloons, remaining firmly canine.

Scooby-Doo

In 1969, another Great Dane appeared on the cartoon scene—Scooby-Doo. Originally envisaged as a minor character in the now-famous TV series about a band of teenage ghostbusters, he took over while the show was still on the drawing board and the working title of *Who's Scared?* became *Scooby-Doo, Where Are You?* In 2002, the first Scooby-Doo movie appeared, shortly followed by a sequel.

Snoopy

World-famous cartoon Beagle Snoopy *(above)* made his debut in the *Peanuts* comic strip in 1950. His creator, Charles M. Schultz, was inspired by his childhood dog Spike. Originally just Charlie Brown's pet, Snoopy evolved into one of the strip's best-loved characters, expressing his views by facial expression and thought balloons and enjoying Walter Mitty daydreams of life as a World War I flying ace.

Sam

Sam the dog and his colleague Max are the stars of Steve Purcell's surrealistic *Sam and Max* comics (and subsequent computer game). Sam, a sad-faced, man-sized hound in a baggy suit, and Max, a "hyperkinetic rabbity thing," are private investigators (or, as they put it, "freelance police") whose adventures take them everywhere from ancient Egypt to the moon, mocking American popular culture as they go.

Not a typical Great Dane, Scooby-Doo has bandy legs, a double chin, and unusual coloring!

DOGS IN ART

On a Grecian urn

The art of Classical Greece depicts dogs ranging from massive guards to dainty pets, but most of its canine imagery celebrates hounds, both streamlined Greyhound types and bulkier packhounds. One vase, from the 5th century B.C., depicts Eros, god of love, accompanied by a hound—not just a companion, but a symbol of the hunt for love, in which the hound will never leave the scent until he captures his quarry.

An amphora dating from the 5th ▶▶ centruy B.C. depicts the winged god Eros accompanied by an alert and graceful dog.

Painter's Pug

Painter and satirist William Hogarth (1697–1764) was inseparable from his Pug dogs. His favorite, Trump, dominates the foreground of his famous self-portrait, and also appears urinating on the works of the poet Churchill in a satirical engraving.

◀◀ Hogarth's painting of Trump records a much leggier, longer-faced, more athletic breed than the chunky modern Pug.

Hogarth himself was caricatured by others as "the author Pugg," while Trump is featured as a charming little porcelain model from the Chelsea pottery factory.

Emblem of fidelity

The little dog in the foreground of Jan van Eyck's *Arnolfini Marriage* (1434) is an emblem of faithfulness in a painting full of marriage symbolism. However, this is also quite recognizably a portrait of a real dog, certainly a valued pet and perhaps belonging to the newly wedded couple. Some see in this little short-muzzled, rough-coated terrier an ancestor of the modern Affenpinscher.

Victorian selection

The Victorians loved pictures that told a story or defined a character. In his *Buy A Dog Ma'am?*, Richard Ansdell (1815–1885) captures for posterity the street corner dogseller, with a splendid selection of dogs to suit all tastes—beribboned lapdogs, stately gundogs, and a little shaggy tyke who looks like a farm worker. Famous for his animal studies, Ansdell also became the only British artist to have a town named after him—Ansdell, in Lancashire.

Sign of status

In the 18th century, well-bred horses and hounds were essential parts of life for the landed gentry, and were often included in paintings. In a celebrated 18th-century equestrian portrait of Sir Roger Burgoyne

(above) by James Seymour (1702–1752), a favorite Foxhound leads the way, moving exactly in pace with the horse. The hound, just as much as the horse and the idealized landscape, acts as an attribute of the country gentleman.

The curly-headed dog boy

Sir Edwin Landseer (1802–1873) loved dogs. He exhibited his first dog painting at the Royal Academy when he was only 13 years old, and went on to become one of the greatest dog painters, producing Victorian favorites like *Jocko with a Hedehog (right)* and his portraits of royal pets. He is the only artist to have given his name to a type of dog: black and white Newfoundlands, of which he was particularly fond, are still known as Landseers.

Matchstick dogs

The famous painter of "matchstick men and matchstick cats and dogs," L.S. Lowry (1887–1976) created an instantly recognizable, simplified, yet lively dog to populate his urban scenes. Oddest is the famous five-legged dog in *Old Church and Steps* (1960). Lowry was surprised when this was pointed out but explained, tongue in cheek, "All I can say is that it must have had five legs. I only paint what I see, you know!"

Sighthound elegance

The combination of dogs and human nudes is a favorite with Lucian Freud (b. 1922), a Whippet owner who appreciates the fluid curves of sighthounds. His own dogs, Pluto and his successor Eli, appear in several paintings, such as *Pluto and the Bateman Sisters*, where Pluto's relaxation counterpoints the more forced pose of the kneeling woman behind him. In *Annabel and Rattler*, an Irish Wolfhound serves the same function.

DOGS IN THE THEATER

Puppet theater

Punch and Judy puppet shows have been part of British street theater since the mid-17th century. Dog Toby, played by a live dog, was introduced into the show in the 18th century. At one time he was such a favorite character that people often spoke of "Punch and Toby" shows. Many Toby dogs not only performed but also collected money after the show. Today, he is usually replaced by a dog puppet.

⬆ *This sketch from 1889 shows Dog Toby wearing his traditional frilly collar. Concerns about mistreatment of performing animals gradually led to his replacement by a puppet.*

Popular performance

The Dog of Montargis, a dramatization of the medieval story of Dragon, the faithful hound who achieved justice for his murdered master, was a 19th-century hit, notching up more than 1,100 performances in Britain alone. Audiences were so enthusiastic that, in 1814, a Dublin theater manager's failure to agree on terms for the canine actor led to two weeks of rioting in the streets!

Shakespearean dog

Shakespeare wrote only one part for a dog in all his works, the comic scene in *Two Gentlemen of Verona* in which clownish servant Launce berates his dog Crab for misbehavior ranging from stealing food to cocking a leg on a lady's skirt. Modern owners of rowdy dogs will sympathize with poor Launce, who has to pretend to have committed all Crab's crimes himself to save his dog from punishment.

A suitably ▶▶ *hangdog Crab, in a production of* Two Gentlemen of Verona *at Regent's Park Open Air Theatre.*

Sadler's Wells star

Performing dogs were all the rage in 19th-century melodramas. At Sadler's Wells Theatre, London, a stage water tank built for depictions of sea battles served splendidly for canine actors to rescue drowning children and sailors. Hero of one such scene was Carlo, former butcher's dog turned actor, whose role in *The Caravan* (1806) made him a national star whose story, *The Life of the Famous Dog Carlo*, was published in 1809.

Getting Goethe's goat

The great German writer Johann Wolfgang von Goethe did not share the public's passion for

Evidently no dog lover, Goethe portrayed the Devil as a Poodle in his play Faust.

performing dogs. In 1817, he walked out of his post as manager of Weimar's State Theatre in disgust when the Duke of Weimar booked Vendredi the Poodle to star in a performance of *The Dog of Montargis*, declaring that he wanted nothing more to do with a theater that permitted dogs on stage.

Terrier triumphs

Other great canine roles include Little Orphan Annie's dog Sandy in the musical *Annie* and Dorothy's dog Toto in *The Wizard of Oz*. A variety of dogs have starred as Sandy and Toto, but terriers stake a claim to the roles. Toto is traditionally a Cairn Terrier and, although Sandy is a sandy-colored, shaggy mongrel, the part has often been played by a Soft-coated Wheaten Terrier.

After being played by the ▶▶ famous Terry in MGM's film, Toto has usually appeared as a Cairn.

Newfoundland nursemaid

One of the most famous roles written for a dog is that of Nana, the canine nursemaid in J.M. Barrie's *Peter Pan*. The character was inspired by Barrie's own dogs, Porthos, a St. Bernard and his successor Luath, a Newfoundland. For the first production, Nana was played by Arthur Lupino, who spent hours studying Luath at home to copy his movements.

Even canine ▶▶ actors have to face ordeal by audition. Here a patient Toby runs through his paces in the hope of securing a part in a London stage production of Chitty Chitty Bang Bang.

Squashed Yorkie

Actress Sarah Miles shared the stage with two of her dogs in her 1999 one-woman show in London, *The Widow Smiles*. Hiawatha the Mastiff disqualified himself by doing a "whirling dervish" act, so only Yorkshire Terriers Batty and Oxton appeared on stage. The show went very well, apart from the moment when Miss Miles accidentally sat on Oxton, who played up to the audience's sympathy like an old ham.

DOGS AND MUSIC

Ancestral voices

Wolves seem to enjoy "singing." They howl to contact pack members or warn neighboring packs of their presence, but group howls seem to be for the pleasure of the sound, each wolf adjusting its pitch to harmonize with the others. Pet dogs generally howl only when lonely—are they calling for company, or are they perhaps singing to comfort themselves?

Quite a few dogs enjoy "singing" along with ⬆ *human music—not always a popular habit, though some harmonize remarkably well.*

Easy listening

So what do dogs think of human music? Research at Queen's University, Belfast, into canine reactions to music showed that dogs were soothed by classical music, indifferent to pop and agitated by heavy metal. Increasingly, dog rescue shelters are using music to relax their inmates, as at the famous Battersea Dogs' Home in London, where a mixture of pop and classical music has proved most successful.

Music critic

Austrian composer Anton Bruckner (1824–1896) was devoted to his Pug, Mops. His mischievous students conditioned the dog to run away if they played music by Wagner, but to expect treats if they played a piece by Bruckner. Then they informed their master that even the dog thought him a better composer than Wagner, and demonstrated how Mops reacted. The innocent Bruckner was delighted!

Singing Pug

In the 1890s, a Pug known by the then acceptable name of Nigger Sam, and owned by Miss Myrtle Stennard-Robinson, became famous as "the Singing Pug," Given a scale on the piano, he picked up the note and let rip with "a short vocal air with marked cadences," a trick he performed to acclaim before titled audiences.

Wagner's cowriters

Composer Richard Wagner (1813–1883) adored his dogs. Two in particular, the spaniel Peps and his successor Fips, played a key part in his

◀◀ *Richard Wagner filled his life with dogs, from huge Newfoundlands to toy spaniels*

◀◀ *You can teach your dog to "play the piano" by rewarding him when he touches the keys, but the result is unlikely to be very pleasing to the ear!*

bows strapped to their paws. Their performance seems to have been impressive, perhaps because Lavater was ahead of his rather brutal time in using humane training methods.

creative routine, occupying a stool beside the piano while he worked. Peps' response to different musical keys (he was excited by E major, but calmed by E-flat major) influenced his master's compositions, while Fips' gambols inspired a passage in the opera *Siegfried*.

Elgar's inspiration

We owe the *Enigma Variations* composed by Sir Edward Elgar (1857–1934), and indeed his *The Dream of Gerontius*, to a clumsy Bulldog! In 1898, Dan the Bulldog fell into the River Wye, Herefordshire, and paddled happily upstream before hauling himself out, barking. His owner, Dr. Sinclair, challenged Elgar to set the incident to music—and he did. In 2002, Dan's contribution was commemorated by a riverside statue and explanatory plaque.

Dog orchestra

In the 19th century Louis Lavater's Dog Orchestra toured Europe with great success. The dogs stood on their hind legs at their instruments (drums, cymbals, violin, bass, and even a trombone), and used drumsticks or

The King and I

Elvis Presley first performed the song *Hound Dog* in 1956, since when it has become irrevocably associated with him. When he sang it on *The Steve Allen Show* later that year, he was asked to tone down his hip-swiveling performance for the TV audience. To be on the safe side, he was provided with a costar to sing to—a top-hatted Basset Hound named Sherlock, who listened solemnly, if a little nervously.

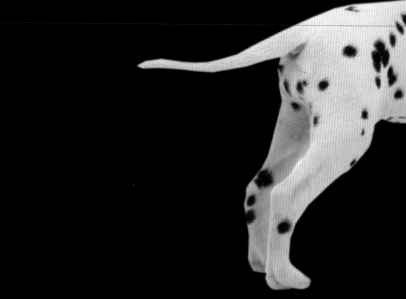

DOGS AND

PEOPLE

DOGS IN OUR LIVES

Coining a phrase

The saying, "A man's best friend is his dog," dates back to a Missouri court in 1870, when Senator George Graham Vest prosecuted Leonidas Hornsby for shooting a hound dog named Old Drum. The famous speech that won his case included the sentence: "The one absolutely unselfish friend that a man can have in this selfish world, the one that never deserts him, the one that never proves ungrateful or treacherous, is his dog."

🔺 *Stroking and talking to a dog helps to reduce stress, lower blood pressure, and activate endorphins ("feel-good hormones").*

heart and liver function by reducing anxiety scores by 24 percent and levels of stress hormone by 17 percent (compared with 10 percent and 2 percent respectively when humans visited alone). The conclusion was that dogs are better for the sick than humans!

Good for dogs?

A recent survey by Britain's The Blue Cross charity suggests that many owners have unrealistic expectations of their dogs—the "Perfect Pet Syndrome." A worrying 75 percent of owners wanted an ideal family dog in exchange for a mere 30 minutes' attention per day, and 87 percent expected a dog to be fully socialized in one month. The idea that a "perfect" dog needs commitment of time and effort seems to have been forgotten.

🔺 *In 1958, a statue of Old Drum was erected outside Warrensburg Courthouse, Missouri.*

Good for people

Researchers studying recovery rates in heart-failure patients compared the beneficial effects of canine visitors versus human ones. They found that a 12-minute canine visit improved

Natural protectors

It isn't just training that makes dogs care about humans. In 1996, a pair of feral dogs came to

the rescue of a young boy lost in the Missouri woods at below-freezing temperatures. After 72 hours, search parties had been almost lost hope of finding ten-year-old Josh Carlisle when the dogs' barking led them to him. Protected from the lethal cold by the dogs' bodies, he survived his ordeal with only slight frostbite.

Support for strays

In 1860, Mrs. Mary Tealby opened a Home for Lost and Starving Dogs in London. The idea was ridiculed at first. "Why not a home for all the starving butterflies and caterpillars of the gardens of London?" jeered *The Times*. But humanitarians, including Charles Dickens, supported the scheme, today a world-famous national institution under its later name of The Battersea Dogs' Home.

⬇ *Today, stray dogs are served by rescue groups worldwide, but there are still more homeless dogs than they can handle.*

A dog's life

A recent survey showed that our modern lifestyle causes our dogs a lot of stress. Veterinarians report an increase in stress-related behavioral problems and ailments from digestive disorders to coat loss. A majority of the dog owners questioned believed stress and anxieties in their own lives affected their pets, while nearly a quarter said they could not spend enough time with their dogs or even provide a daily walk.

⬆ *Stressed dogs may engage in self-harming activities like obsessive tail-chasing.*

Progress?

Ancient Greek author Plutarch ruled, "A good man will take care of his horses and dogs, not only while they are young, but when they are old and past service"; 2000 years later, people's reasons for giving unwanted dogs to rescue societies include: "He doesn't match my new sofa," "She hurts my legs when she wags her tail," and, of course, "I'm going on vacation."

DOG-LOVERS

King Charles II

Notorious for "playing with his dogs all the while, and not minding his business," Charles II (1630–1885) took great delight in the toy spaniels that bear his name today. At a time when royal courts were notoriously squalid, diarist John Evelyn commented that the King's dogs "made the whole court nasty and stinking," especially the royal bedchamber.

⬆ *Even when receiving the first pineapple grown in England, Charles was attended by his dogs.*

Sir Walter Scott

Dogs were the best friends of novelist Sir Walter Scott (1771–1832). Camp the Bull Terrier, Ginger and Spice the Dandie Dinmonts, and a series of Greyhounds and Deerhounds shared his life, but it was Maida, a huge, dignified

Sir Walter Scott valued the dog as the ▸▸ *"companion of our pleasures and our toils… with a nature noble and incapable of deceit."*

Deerhound-Mastiff cross, that was most famous. Maida sat for his portrait so many times that, Scott said, he would stalk off in disgust at the sight of a painter's gear.

General George Custer

U.S. cavalry commander George Custer (1839–1876) was inseparable from his racing Greyhounds, including his favorite, Tuck, who despite her size, insisted on sleeping on his lap, and the lordly Byron, who used to push the general's wife out of bed to make room for himself. One of Custer's last actions before the Battle of Little Bighorn, where he and all his men died, was to send his beloved dogs away to safety.

Lord George Gordon Byron

Romantic poet Lord Byron (1788–1824) *(left)* favored large dogs, including Mastiffs, Bulldogs, and even a wolf hybrid, though the latter was distinctly unreliable and, Byron records, "very nearly ate me." His favorites were Newfoundlands, notably Boatswain, beloved dog of his youth, whose epitaph says he had "all the virtues of man without his vices," and Lyon, constant companion of his last days.

No disciplinarian

Novelist Thomas Hardy (1840–1928) loved his dog Wessex dearly, but few others did. The spoiled Fox Terrier, who supervised Hardy's writings from a comforter in his study, was a household tyrant that bit guests (except, for some reason, Lawrence of Arabia, whom he liked) and had to be shut away when the Prince of Wales called. But Hardy and his wife Florence excused every fault of their "devoted and masterful" dog.

David Hockney

Dachshunds are the favorites of British artist David Hockney (b.1937), who enjoys the company of a pair named Stanley and Boodgie. In 1995, he exhibited a set of 45 paintings of his canine friends. They are typically depicted snoozing, for practical reasons, when awake, he says, they are "not very good models. One knock on the door is enough to make them leap up."

P.G. Wodehouse

A lifelong addiction to Pekingeses characterized the comic writer P.G. Wodehouse (1881–1975) *(above)*. This landed him in trouble in World War II, when a reluctance to put his Peke Wonder into quarantine left him in France, where he became a prisoner of war and later faced accusations of Nazi sympathies. It didn't put him off Pekes: in middle age he was described as appearing "to wade in a sea of Pekingese."

⬆ *Actor Humphrey Bogart (1899–1957) was famed for his "tough guy" roles, but he was very attached to his dogs. Here his Scottish Terrier Sluggy poses for a photograph.*

DOGS AND FASHION

Status symbols

Since ancient times, certain breeds have been recognized as status symbols. Rich people's companions were big dogs such as Mastiffs and Greyhounds or tiny dogs such as Maltese and Pugs; medium-sized mongrels never made it into the fashion charts. Today, dogs are still often chosen for their image. Why else does a confirmed couch potato buy a Siberian Husky designed to run 100 miles (160 km) a day, or a Shih Tzu that needs hours of grooming?

Class-conscious choices

An old verse linking various sporting breeds to classes in life prescribes the Flat-coated Retriever for gamekeepers and the extinct Norfolk Spaniel for farmers ("or the parson if he shoots"), concluding "But, over all the common curs, A setter for the squire." The writer also mentions terriers "for the labourer And other simple folk." What would he have thought of Prince Charles' predilection for Jack Russells?

Celebrity craze

Chihuahuas are the "must-have" fashion statements for modern celebrities, including Madonna, Paris Hilton, and Britney Spears. Dressed up like dolls in cashmere sweaters,

⚑ *Living creatures need a lot more care than most fashion accessories, and run the risk of outliving their owner's interest.*

mink coats, or even tennis shoes, the little dogs appear at every photo opportunity, often to be discarded when the novelty wears off. Being a living fashion accessory really is a dog's life!

Handbag horrors

In 2005, the RSPCA (Royal Society for the Prevention of Cruelty to Animals) felt obliged to warn against the latest craze for carrying little dogs around in designer handbags, pointing out that dogs are meant to walk. Behaviorists also cautioned that dogs who spend long periods riding in a bag don't get enough

⚑ *A spiked red velvet collar for a trendy dog. Designer collars for the dogs of dedicated followers of fashion come in every style from punk to Art Nouveau, with adornments ranging from rhinestones to real diamonds.*

into floor-length twisted ropes, or the fashion for dyeing them pastel shades, which was popular in the 1980s and is currently enjoying a revival.

↥ *He looks cute peeping out of a handbag, but it's not a suitable lifestyle for a dog.*

contact with the outside world and can become stressed and aggressive.

They call them toys…

Toy breeds have traditionally been fashion favorites—or fashion victims, treated as accessories, not animals. Saki (H.H. Munro) satirized this trend in his short story *Louis* (1919), in which selfish Lena Strudwarden gets her own way by pleading the needs of her spoiled Pomeranian, Louis, until her husband discovers the dog is only a lifelike toy, for his wife "disliked animals, but liked getting her own way under a halo of unselfishness."

Clips and colors

The Poodle's dense, nonshedding coat lends itself to fashion extravaganzas. The modern show Poodle's lion clip may seem somewhat extreme, but some 18th-century owners even had their coats of arms cut into their dogs' fur. Equally bizarre was the fad for cording coats

Canine couture

For those who want to accessorize their accessories, *haute couture* for dogs has arrived *(four photos above)*. Top designers such as Gucci, Burberry, Prada, Ralph Lauren, and Chanel now supply clothing for dogs, from pajamas to baseball caps and from slogan T-shirts to sunglasses. Other ranges include nail polish, fur highlighters, deodorants, and canine colognes—rolling in eau de skunk is just so yesterday!

LIFESAVERS

Mountain hero

Barry was the most famous of the mountain rescue dogs of St. Bernard's Hospice, in the Swiss Alps. He is credited with saving the lives of 40 snowbound travelers

between 1800 and 1812. Legend says he was killed trying to save a forty-first, who mistook him for a wolf and stabbed him, but it is probable that he died of old age after a comfortable two years' retirement in Berne.

◄◄ *Barry's heroic death is probably fictional but to this day the Hospice honors his genuine feats by always naming one of its dogs Barry.*

Dockside hero

Jack, a Flat-coated Retriever that lived in Swansea, Wales, in the 1930s, appointed himself lifesaver at the docks. During his lifetime, he rescued 27 people from drowning, collected large amounts of money for charity, and became a national hero. He received numerous awards and in 1936 was named "The Star Bravest Dog of the Year." Today, a stone memorial to Swansea Jack stands on the sea front.

Jellybean heroine

Sometimes saving a life demands brains rather than bravery; In 1996, when Roz Brown of

Cambridge, England, fell into a diabetic coma, her West Highland White Terrier Holly raced to fetch jellybeans, which she placed by her mistress's mouth before nudging her into consciousness. Somehow Holly realized that Roz needed to eat, and sure enough, the sweets revived her enough for her to stagger to the kitchen.

River rescue

Tarka the Labrador was awarded the 1995 U.K. PRO Dog Gold Medal after she saved a canine friend. When Poppy, a Yorkshire Terrier puppy, fell into a freezing river and was swept away, Tarka leapt unhesitatingly after her. Owner Julie Webb watched in horror as both dogs disappeared under the water. A few moments later, Tarka emerged with Poppy in her mouth and carried her safely to the riverbank.

Labradors are ►► strong swimmers, but Tarka risked her own life to rescue Poppy from drowning.

Hearing dog plus

Bertie the Yorkshire Terrier, hearing dog of Gill Stevenson of Aberystwyth, Wales, behaved as impeccably as usual when his owner went into the hospital for a few days in 2001, spending visiting hours curled up quietly on her feet. Luckily, he was still on the alert. Suddenly he started barking frantically at the patient in the next bed, just in time to alert nurses that she had stopped breathing and to save her life.

⬆ *Tess the Labrador receives a hug from Arron Whines at the Superdog Awards 1991. She saved the life of the toddler when she found him lying facedown in a rockpool.*

Ordeal by alligator

Few dogs have faced down an alligator, but Blue, an Australian Blue Heeler living in Florida, did just that in defense of his 85-year-old mistress who lay helpless after a fall. When a hungry alligator approached her, Blue attacked it and managed to drive it off, despite suffering multiple puncture wounds and a gash in his stomach. His courage won him a Dog Hero of the Year award for 2001.

Facing the fire

In 1985, Nipper the sheepdog rushed into a blazing barn to rescue the 300 sheep and their lambs trapped inside. Despite thick smoke and flames, he located the panicked animals and drove them out to safety. Then, ignoring his own burned paws and smoke-filled lungs, he went back for cattle housed at the far end of the barn. Nipper's courage was recognized with the U.K. PRO Dogs Award for devotion to duty.

BAD DOGS

Wily watchdog

Security guards at a Yugoslavian factory were baffled by a thief who eluded watchdog Dzeki to steal thousands of dollars worth of copper rolls in nightly raids. All was explained when a hidden camera showed Dzeki herself sneaking off to raid the stores, then burying her loot in the grounds. Most of her stash was located with a metal detector, and Dzeki was allowed to keep her job— after the storeroom was dog-proofed.

Gundog goes shooting

An English Setter puppy named Sonny started his hunting career on a big scale in 2002, when he accompanied his master Michael Murray on the first day of the hunting season in South Dakota. Murray and his friends were posing for a photo with the birds they had shot, when Sonny stepped on the trigger of a loaded shotgun—and shot his master. Fortunately, it was only an ankle wound.

⬆ *Harvey's escapade landed Johnny Vaughan with the bill—the insurance company refused to pay out since Harvey was not a listed driver*

Bad driving

No sooner had TV presenter Johnny Vaughan gotten out of his Maserati sports car than his bulldog Harvey jumped into the driver's seat. Catching the gearstick on his way up, Harvey knocked the car into gear and then, jumping down into the well, landed on the accelerator. The car shot forward, and Harvey "drove" it into a parked van, wreaking some $20,000 worth of damage.

Contempt of court?

In January 2002, Newcastle Crown Court in England had to adjourn the trial of a man accused of aggravated burglary, because a dog had eaten a key exhibit. An embarrassed defense lawyer explained that while he was looking after a friend's Bullmastiff, Nalla, she had chewed up the closed circuit

television video, which was vital evidence. Many dog owners will recognize the words, "She had never chewed anything before…"

Mailmen in peril

It's understandable that many dogs distrust mailmen—from a canine point of view, they are suspicious characters who are never invited in! It's equally understandable that mailmen object to being bitten by irresponsible owners' dogs. However, the ferocious dog that shut down mail delivery to an entire street in Hobart, Indiana, caused some amusement in the press: Bobo was a 4½-pound (2-kg) Chihuahua.

⬆ *Protect your mailman! In the U.K., postal workers report 5,000 dog attacks annually, with the loss of 4,500 working days per year.*

Moneygrabber

Bull Terriers are notorious for eating things they shouldn't, but six-year-old Tassila from Sweden went too far when she gobbled up two 500 crown bills (worth about $100). Owner Gunilla Gonon-Sabelstrom watched her pet like a hawk until nature took its course and the bills reappeared. She was quoted as saying, "They are slightly yellow, and I think I'll iron them…"

Demolition expert

Twelve-year-old Holly, a black Labrador, was the winner in the Most Destructive Dog in Britain competition. A rescue dog suffering from separation anxiety, she did so much damage to her owners' car that they had to buy her an old Ford Fiesta of her own to sleep in. Having restyled the interior by eating most of it, Holly now loves her den on wheels—and when she wants attention, she beeps the horn with her nose.

She looks as if butter wouldn't ▶▶ *melt in her mouth, but Holly the Labrador is an award-winning amateur car wrecker!*

A lucky trip

Man's best friend can sometimes be an obstacle in his path: "tripping over the family dog" is not an uncommon cause in accident statistics. However, when John Lawrence, who had been blind for four years, tripped over his guide dog on the stairs, he ended up being grateful. As he fell, he hit his head, and regained his sight, presumably having jarred his optic nerve in just the right way.

Insurers report that the most ▶▶ *common canine accidents include swallowing toys, running away from the veterinarian, and getting their heads stuck in cat doors, a mistake that often means owners have to buy a new door.*

DOG EQUIPMENT

Choosing a collar

Prospective buyers are faced with a bewildering array of collars, headcollars, and harnesses, but a simple rolled leather collar serves most purposes. Check chains are not recommended; incorrectly used, they can live up to their old name of "choke chains" and cause both pain and lasting injury. Some dogs are happier with a harness, while a headcollar is a gentle and effective means of re-training a confirmed puller.

◄◄ Collars should be practical, durable, and fit comfortably. A sturdy buckle is much safer than a quick-release plastic fastening.

heavy chains that weigh down the collar. Extending leads are useful if correctly used; if not, they can trip up other walkers or snap into legs, and they should never be used when a dog can dash into traffic.

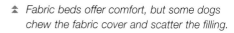

Choosing a leash

Even an item as simple as a leash comes in many varieties. Look for one with a secure catch that won't give way if your dog pulls. Lightweight leads, so long as they are strong enough for the dog in question, are better than

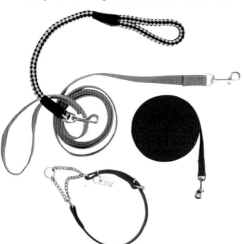

▲ Fabric beds offer comfort, but some dogs chew the fabric cover and scatter the filling.

Beds

Dogs appreciate comfort, but an expensive bed may be spurned if it's put in the wrong place: choose a draft-free place that affords peace and privacy. Wicker baskets look attractive, but are not a good idea with teething puppies or confirmed chewers! Fiberglass beds are easily cleaned, raised beds often appreciated, and cozy igloos ideal for tiny dogs. Elaborate four-posters appeal more to owners than to dogs!

Dog doors

A dog flap giving access to the garden helps dogs to be clean in the house and saves owners standing by on doorman duty. Dog doors come in various sizes, although you need to consider

▲ Leashes of different lengths and long lines are suitable for different purposes. The double-action check collar is popular for show use.

he fact that larger ones may be big enough to admit a burglar. Doors should be lockable from either side to give the option of shutting your dog in or out, and sturdy enough to withstand a urry body hurtling through at top speed.

The right toys

Most dogs love toys, and their owners often get as much pleasure as they give in providing a variety of playthings. Not all toys sold for pets are safe, however. Some are too small, so a dog may choke on them or swallow them. Others aren't tough enough to stand up to chewing (especially if you own a strong-jawed dog such as a Bull Terrier), and again, parts may be swallowed. Always play safe, and choose toys with care.

◀◀ *Buy only balls that are big enough for your dog, many dogs need a trip to the veterinarian after swallowing small toys.*

Better bowls

For reasons of hygiene, dogs need their own food and water bowls. There is a wide choice of pottery, plastic, or stainless steel bowls to suit all tastes. Avoid combination bowls designed to serve both food and water, as one usually tips into the other. Special stands to raise bowls above the ground *(right)* are recommended or big or elderly dogs, to make eating easier.

▲ *A crate can be a valuable training aid, but should never be treated as a "lockup."*

Crates and gates

A crate provides your dog with a cozy den where he can have time out from household hubbub; it also helps to speed housetraining, as he won't want to soil his bed, and can be used to make travel safer. If your puppy is introduced to his crate properly, he will appreciate having his own space. Dog gates are also a valuable training aid, enabling you to restrict your pet's access to parts of the house until he knows how to behave.

Hygiene

Dogs, like children, can be messy creatures. You will need a good supply of old towels to wipe muddy feet, as well as suitable grooming equipment to keep fur clean and in good condition (and to remove mud, dead leaves, or worse after country walks). You will also—almost certainly—need a good flea spray, or rather two—one for the dog, and one to treat carpets and furniture to prevent the fleas from settling in.

DOG ACCESSORIES TO MAKE

Toys for free

You can make great dog toys for free out of household bits and pieces, so long as you bear in mind the destructive capacities of particular breeds—and individuals. Cardboard toilet roll tubes will give a gentle toy breed hours of amusement, and empty plastic bottles make great throw-around toys for a bigger dog. However, strong-jawed breeds such as Bull Terriers need durable toys they can't chew up and swallow.

Winter woollies (big dogs)

Recycle your old sweater to keep your large size Labrador warm in winter. Measure his length from the base of the neck to the end of the rib cage, and cut the sweater to that length. Shorten the sleeves to fall about halfway down his forelegs. Bind all raw edges with bias binding, and you have a snuggly sweater— for free.

⬆ *An old towel makes a great tug toy, but won't stand very much of this usage!*

Tough tug toys

Most dogs enjoy tug toys, which can be made at home. Most types of rope are best avoided, as constant chewing can lead to a dog ingesting fibers. For medium-sized dogs up, you can make a strong, safe tug toy by cutting off the leg of an old pair of jeans and tying it in a knot. This will stand up to all but the most resolute chewers.

⬆ *Old soft toys can be recycled for puppies, but check for small parts that could be swallowed, and beware loose stuffing.*

Bed warmer (small dogs)

Materials:

Two 10-inch (25-cm) squares of sturdy fabric such as denim
Cotton-thread
Small bag of bran or oatmeal
Teaspoonful of dried lavender

Method:

Lay the fabric squares on top of each other and stitch them together along three sides, leaving a 0.25-inch (6-mm) border. Stitch each end of the fourth side, leaving a gap in the center. Turn inside out to form a bag, and stuff loosely with the bran or oatmeal and lavender before stitching up the opening. Warm the bag in the microwave for one to two minutes until it is pleasantly warm but not too hot, and place in your dog's bed as a safe alternative to a hot water bottle. Not recommended for chewers!

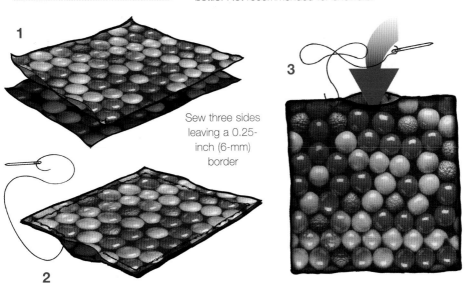

1

Sew three sides leaving a 0.25-inch (6-mm) border

2

3

DIET

What's for dinner?

Dogs are omnivores that can thrive on a wide variety of diets. Until postwar years, most were fed on scraps. Today, we are spoiled for choice with a huge range of commercial dog foods, including special diets for different age ranges, vegetarian, and even calorie-controlled meals. Some think the whole business has gone too far and recommend a return to a "BARF" ("bones and raw food") menu.

Mistaken appetite

Veterinarians regularly see canine patients that have eaten socks, stones, or, in the case of a German Shepherd named Libby, 28 golf balls! A Springer Spaniel named Belle ate more than 600 pebbles with a combined weight of more than 3 pounds (1.4 kg). Kyle, a six-month-old crossbred puppy, outdid them all by swallowing a 15-inch (38-cm) serrated knife only 3 inches (7.6 cm) shorter than himself—and yes, after surgery he was as good as new.

Fat Fido

Many veterinarians feel that obesity—blamed on lack of exercise and overfeeding—is the number one killer of dogs in the West. Studies suggest that nearly half the dogs in the U.S. and U.K. are overweight. Fat dogs age faster and die younger than slim ones. They enjoy life less and cost more in veterinary bills, so it makes sense to ignore those pleading eyes and ration the treats.

Dalmatian on a diet

Harley the Dalmatian was hailed as "the fattest dog in Britain" when he came into rescue care in 2002. Overfeeding by his misguided elderly owner had turned him into a 155-pound (70-kg) lump that couldn't even make it as a couch potato because he was too fat to climb onto the couch. After new owners and a crash diet reduced his weight to 84 pounds (38 kg), the seven-year-old was transformed into "a big puppy" full of energy.

How much food?

A dog's nutritional needs depend on its size, breed, and lifestyle. At one extreme, a 5-pound (2.3-kg) Chihuahua enjoying moderate exercise (one or two hours a day) needs about 250 calories per day. At the other end, a racing Husky needs a lot of fuel to haul a sled 150 miles (240 km) a day—a daily regimen of up to 10,000 calories during a race is required.

⌃ *Dogs do best if mealtimes are scheduled to a regular routine, whether you serve one meal a day or divide the daily ration into two or more meals. Don't forget to take into account treats and tidbits when calculating how much food your dog receives each day.*

⚠ *To check your dog's weight, weigh yourself first, then stand on the scale holding your dog and deduct the difference in weight.*

Obesity test

You don't need scales to judge whether your dog is overweight, just a pair of eyes. On a fit dog, you can see (and feel) the outline of the ribs. Viewed from above, he has a perceptible waist; viewed from the side, his belly is tucked up higher than his ribcage. (Breeds vary in the amount of "tuck-up"; it is most pronounced in Greyhound types.) Highly visible ribs mean a dog is too thin; no waist or tuck-up means he is too fat.

Tricks with treats

Food treats make great training aids, but little and often can add inches to a dog's waistline. Some dogs will work happily for low-calorie treats such as pieces of raw carrot or apple, but others insist on more fattening treats. One way around this problem is to divide up a dog's daily ration into tiny portions (easier done with a dry-food diet) and use these as rewards during training sessions instead of serving a main meal.

⚠ *Food treats are valuable training aids, but too many treats can harm your dog's health.*

Hazardous foods

Chocolate is toxic to dogs, dark chocolate being the most dangerous. As little as 8 ounces (225 g) can be a fatal dose for a small dog. Most dogs find chocolate irresistible, so keep this treat well out of their reach. Other foods to avoid include onions, raisins, grapes, and raw potatoes, all of which can cause serious health problems if eaten in large quantities.

COOKING FOR DOGS

MAIN COURSES

Lamb and rice

- 1 pound (450 g) minced lamb
- 8 ounces (225 g) brown rice
- 1 large carrot, grated
- 7 ounces (200 g) plain yogurt
- 1 clove garlic, finely chopped

⏶ *Most dogs take a great interest in their food, and are more likely to need to be prevented from overeating than to be tempted to eat enough. If your dog lacks appetite, try fasting him for a day instead of offering treats.*

Mix the lamb and garlic, place in pan with water, and cook over a low heat, covered, until tender. Drain, and mix with other ingredients except the yogurt. Allow to cool, stir in yogurt, and serve a portion suitable to the size of your dog.

Microwave casserole

- 1 pound (450 g) gravy beef, diced
- 4 ounces (110 g) sliced green beans
- 1 large carrot, finely chopped
- 1 stick celery, sliced
- 1 teaspoon beef extract

Place all ingredients in a microwable dish, cover with water, and mix. Cover dish, and microwave on high for 10 minutes, then medium for another 10 minutes. Allow to cool for an hour before serving a suitable portion.

Low-fat dieter's delight

- 1 pound (450 g) lean chopped beef
- 2 large carrots, chopped
- 4 ounces (110 g) mixed cooked greens
- 1 pound (450 g) low-fat cottage cheese
- Low-fat cooking spray

Lightly brown beef in cooking spray. Drain off any fat, and mix beef with remaining ingredients. Allow to cool before serving suitable portion.

Treats

Doggy treats are often designed to please owners as much as dogs. Most dogs are happy to eat items we may consider inedible!

Doggy birthday cake

1 pound (450 g) lean chopped beef
8 ounces (225 g) oatmeal
4 ounces (110 g) biscuit crumbs

Pre-heat oven to 350°F. Blend all ingredients in an electric blender, pour into a greased oblong cake tin and bake for 25-35 minutes. Allow to cool before inverting on to a plate. Top with nonfat sour cream or mashed potato for a healthy "icing."

Cheese and garlic biscuits

12 ounces (340 g) wholemeal flour
12 ounces (340 g) grated cheese
8 ounces (225 g) margarine
1 clove garlic, crushed
Milk to mix

Cream together all ingredients except the milk, then gradually add milk a little at a time until the mixture forms a ball. Chill for 30 minutes, then roll out on a floured board and cut into shapes (two to three dozen, depending on size). Bake at 350°F for 15 minutes until lightly browned.

Liver treats

1 pound (450 g) liver
8 ounces (225 g) wholemeal flour
4 ounces (110 g) oatmeal
4 ounces (110 g) cornmeal
2 eggs

 Don't serve all the biscuits at once, or your pet will need to go on a hasty diet.

Blend liver in an electric blender until it forms a soft paste. Put all the other ingredients into a bowl, add the liver, and blend together. Pour into a greased baking tin and bake at 300°F for 30 minutes. When cool, cut into bite-sized pieces. These treats will keep in the refrigerator for up to a week, or can be frozen.

THE DOG-FRIENDLY GARDEN

Planning and patience

Some say that dogs and gardens don't mix, but of course they do—it just takes planning and patience. You may have to adjust your gardening style in favor of durability; dense planting helps, and fragile plants may need protection. You will certainly have to spend time on training. A puppy left alone and uninstructed in the garden will amuse himself somehow, usually with demolition work.

Dogs enjoy a garden to explore, and planning ▶▶ ahead will ensure that no harm comes to either.

SAFETY TIPS	
HAZARD	**PRECAUTION**
Sharp-edged tools	Store out of pets' reach and always put away after use.
Garden chemicals (fertilizers, weed-killers, etc.)	Store out of pets' reach and avoid using in areas where your dog goes.
Electric cables	Make sure these are out of reach or otherwise protected to prevent chewing.
Lawn mowers, trimmers, etc.	Always keep an eye on your dog when using these. A moment's inattention can lead to serious injury.
Ponds/Pools	Fencing and supervision needed with puppies and heavily built breeds such as French Bulldogs and Bassets, which tend to sink rather than swim. Training sessions advisable to keep dogs on dry land in garden, to prevent damage to pond, and water everywhere.
Planting	Avoid thorny and spiny plants, which can cause eye injuries. Most dogs are too sensible to eat poisonous plants, but bulbs may be tempting, so take care.
Mulches	Choose mulches carefully. Cocoa mulch is popular but poisonous, and dangerously attractive to dogs.

Border patrols

Dogs like to patrol their territory, and it's not uncommon for paws to wear a path across the lawn or borders. Providing suitable paths where they can walk without doing any damage is one way; perimeter routes are usually appreciated, and can be screened by sturdy planting. Where a dog has already established a favorite route, it may be easiest to give in and lay steppingstones.

Digging

Gardeners and dogs both dig, but when dogs do it, they can wreck a garden. Some individuals, and indeed, some breeds, such as terriers, are digging addicts. Providing a "sand-pit" where digging is allowed, and training your dog not to delve elsewhere, is one possible solution; another is to make sure he has something else to do (try a food-stuffed toy) when he is in the garden. With confirmed miners, constant supervision may be the only answer.

⬟ *Dogs dig to bury bones, explore mouse-holes, scrape out a bed, or just for sheer fun.*

Sun and shade

Dogs often enjoy lying in the sun *(right)*, but make sure that shade is always available, whether a purposely built shelter or just some handy bushes. Short-faced breeds in particular can easily overheat, and (like human sunbathers) may not always have the sense to move out of the sun in time, so supervise their yard time on hot days.

Hygiene matters

How do you save your garden from turning into a canine toilet? One method is to "'garden-train" your dog, teaching him not to eliminate there; this means frequent walks, prepared with pooper-scoopers. Another is to teach him to use a designated and easily cleaned toilet area in one corner. Otherwise, you can simply do as you would on a walk and pick up after your pet each time you let him out.

Lawn problems

Brown patches on the lawn can be caused by dogs' urine. Bitches are usually to blame; male dogs more often lift a leg on a tree than soil the lawn. The damage can be prevented by immediately watering the area to dilute the urine, but it may be easier to cordon off sections to give them time to recover. Failing that, try replanting with a tougher grass such as fescue.

DOG COLLECTIBLES

Postage stamps

Stamps featuring dogs must be among the most attractive of small and affordable dog collectibles. More than 4,000 different dog stamps have appeared since the first was issued in 1877 in Newfoundland, featuring, naturally, a Newfoundland dog. Subjects range from Laika, first dog in space, and Chinese Year of the Dog commemorative issues to breed studies and cartoon dogs.

Dog collars

Historic dog collars are highly collectible and range from lapdogs' beadwork necklets to fearsome medieval spiked collars made to protect hounds' throats when fighting wolves, bears, or wild boars. Elaborate 18th-century collars might bear owners' coats of arms, while a century later the dogs of the rich boasted engraved silver collars and common dogs wore brass collars fastened with a padlock.

▲ *China collectors aren't just limited to figurines, but can seek out unusual items such as this 20th-century German Dachshund teapot.*

▲ *This silver and garnet collar bearing the Conti family crest is likely to carry a price tag beyond the means of many amateur collectors.*

China and pottery

Ceramic dogs come in a range to suit every taste and every pocket, from rare Chinese porcelain to 18th-century "pot dogs" and modern realistic breed models. Staffordshire dogs are popular collectibles, notably the pairs of "comforter" spaniels that guarded so many Victorian mantelpieces, as well as elegant stylized Greyhounds and jolly spotted Dalmatians.

Furry friends

Vintage stuffed toys are rare, most having been literally loved to pieces by their young owners, but today's toys are tomorrow's collectibles. The famous German firm of Steiff has been producing dogs as soft toys since the early 1900s. Their very rare, and very expensive, early

models are appealingly naïve; their modern range includes breeds from Afghan Hound to Schnauzer.

This unusual ceramic group reveals the ⬆ motif of Greyhounds and elegant women so beloved of Art Deco designers.

message around the picture on the other side. In 1902, the postcard really took off, following the bright idea of dividing the space on the back of the card to accommodate both message and address. Since then the range of dog postcards has been endless!

Deco dogs

In the 1920s and '30s, the stylish lines of Greyhounds and Borzois took the fancy of Art Deco designers. Posters, jewelery, and bronzes of the period feature a horde of leggy hounds, often accompanying equally svelte women, while streamlined cars boasted equally streamlined Greyhound mascots. Art Deco Greyhounds are as expensive as they are attractive, but more affordable modern reproductions abound.

Dog jewelry

Dogs have inspired an incredible range of jewelry—brooches, earrings, pins, and pendants in every material from gold to plastic and in every style from the elegant to the tacky. Modern jewelers produce meticulously detailed gold or silver dogs of practically every known breed, as well as delightful ranges in pewter for budget buyers.

Postcards

Picture postcards were invented in 1870, although at first one side was reserved for the address and senders had to squeeze in their

⬆ *Today, cushions depict almost every breed. This attractive example features a Sealyham.*

Needlework dogs

The 19th-century craze for Berlin woolwork produced many appealing needlepoint dogs; portraits of Queen Victoria's spaniel Dash being a favorite. Several modern designers have produced charts to enable modern stitchers to sew similar pieces. Sewing tools—thimbles, pincushions, needlecases, or tape-measures—also often feature dogs and make delightful collectibles.

DOG COLLECTIBLES

Character dogs

A whole range of collectibles features famous canines—fictional dogs such as Lassie, cartoon dogs such as Disney's Lady and the Tramp, and real-life figures from presidential pets to notable racing Greyhounds. Disney's Pluto is said to appear on more memorabilia than any other dog in the world, rare 1930s products being most highly valued, while more recently, Charles Schultz's Snoopy looks to be catching up with him.

Paper ephemera

The 19th century saw a plethora of printed and embossed paper "scraps" for scrapbooks, which include dogs and puppies galore. Other collectable canine ephemera include advertisements, cigar bands, calendars, greetings cards, match-box labels, and posters. Dogs are also well represented on trade cards, with everything from photos to the work of famous illustrators such as Arthur Wardle.

Rabbits, I Believe?

▲ *Some Foo Dogs are Pekingese in light disguise; others are grotesquely dragonlike.*

◀◀ *A 1920s postcard depicts two little dogs wreaking havoc on the golf course.*

Foo Dogs

Lovers of Oriental dogs may be attracted by Chinese Foo Dogs. Originating as statues of lions set outside palaces, tombs, and official buildings, these later became stylized into lion dogs resembling the "lion dog" we know as the

Pekingese. Collectors will find ceramic, jade, wooden, and metal statuettes available today, usually in pairs, the male holding a ball and the female a puppy.

Wood carvings

Some of the most enchanting carved dogs are Japanese *netsuke*, miniature masterpieces both old and modern. Antiques from walking-sticks to inkwells also feature dogs, and collectors can also look out for canine bookends, candle-sticks, or children's toys. Today, carved dogs are produced all over the world, ranging from breed studies by special woodcarvers to naïve folk art—something for everyone.

Metalware

Metal dogs can be found in forms ranging from cast-iron lockboxes and clockwork tinplate toys to horse brasses and finely detailed bronze

statuettes. There is some-thing for everyone, whether you specialize in a particular style or sculptor, or choose to build up a collection of your favorite breed modeled as letter openers, door-knockers, or whatever you can find.

Metal toys are eminently collectible, whether simple models (left) or mechanical toys like the "trick dog" moneybox (right).

Scottie selection

Scottish terriers, with their characteristically geometric outline, have long been a favorite theme for designers. Scottie collectors can find anything from kitsch to class—vintage brasses, Art Deco brooches, Black Forest woodcarvings, models of President Roosevelt's Fala, and bizarre Japanese models with black and white stripes, the result, apparently, of mistranslating the term "brindle."

Dog books

Building up a collection of books on a favorite breed can be a challenging hobby. Rare older titles can be located through specialized dealers, but there is great satisfaction to be had in locating a prize at garage sales or thrift shops. As well as the standard guides, don't forget to keep an eye out for fiction, children's stories, and breed club yearbooks, some of which are rare and much in demand.

Badges and medals

There is growing interest in collecting dog badges and medals. Jewelers produce attractive breed portrait badges in pewter or precious metals. For serious collectors, vintage dog club badges fetch high prices, while current versions are the collectibles of the future. The same is true of medals, whether awards for heroism or show prizes, the older examples being rare and highly prized.

Canine collectible glassware includes various styles of models made of blown glass, stained glass panels, mosaic pictures, etched goblets, and more elaborate pieces such as this Italian glass and silver decanter, dating from the 1920s.

AN ORIGAMI DOG—MAKING THE HEAD

Origami is the Japanese art of folding paper to make cleverly shaped models, such as flowers, birds, or animals. This cute dog creation is made of two separate sections. No scissors or glue needed, just careful, accurate folds.

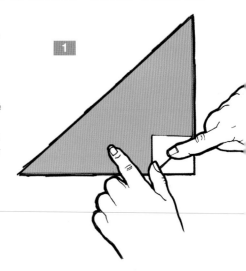

1 Begin with a square of paper. Make a crease diagonally along the center line from corner to corner. The paper will now be in the shape of a right-angle triangle. Fold over the bottom corner as illustrated; this forms the dog's nose.

2 Fold the two pointed corners obliquely inward. They project over the top of the model to form the ears.

3 The next stage requires you to squash fold the tops of the ears downward. By applying pressure (green arrow), the paper will open out and squash flat.

4 This is how you make the fold described in Stage 3. Notice how the ear section is opening out as it is folded down.

5 The finished head section with both ears completed should look like this.

6 Now decorate the head by sticking on two circular adhesive labels to make the eyes. Use a marker pen to draw in the pupils and add an appealing little button-shaped nose, smiling mouth, and whiskers.

Why not...

Use differently colored papers of different sizes to create an entire family of fun dogs and puppies? Single colors, Spaniel patches, Dalmatian spots—the choice is yours.

DOG BIZ

For instructions on how to make the dog's body, see overleaf

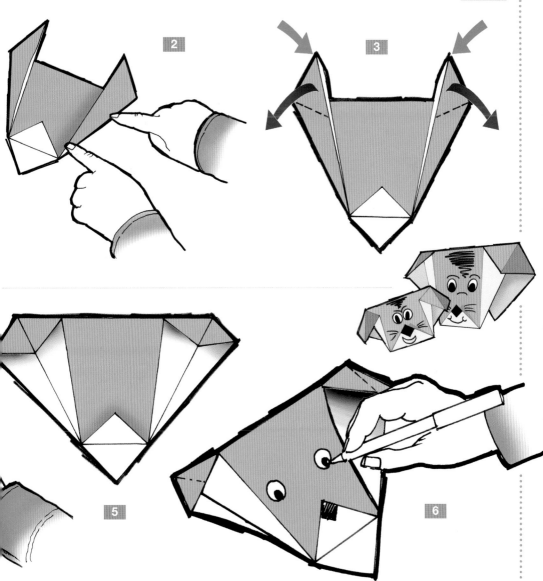

163

AN ORIGAMI DOG—MAKING THE BODY

The dog's body is quite straightforward to make. The folds at Stage 5 require a little dexterity as you squash the corners in, but practice makes perfect.

1 Again, start with a square of paper in a diamond position. This drawing shows the three folds that you will make initially.

2 Fold the left- and right-hand sides in. Note that the edges of the paper do not meet on the center line; they stop short and run parallel to it. The lower triangular section is then folded behind so that it is out of view.

3 Your paper should now look like this. The next step is to fold the top over and to sink the two corners in with inside reverse folds as shown in Stages **4** and **5**.

4 This is simple. Fold the tip of the model behind so that the "legs" run right to the top.

5 Now crease the bottom corners obliquely at an angle (see drawing for Stage **3**), unfold them again and apply pressure to the outer edges (green arrows). The two corners will sink inward as illustrated. This provides the stable base on which the model sits.

Finishing touches

Again, a marker pen can be used to draw some little paws and distinctive markings on the body section that you have just made. Now all you need to do is to perch the head section on the body and your canine charmer will be smiling back at you! By altering the angle at which you sit the head on the body, you can even get one dog to "look" at the other.

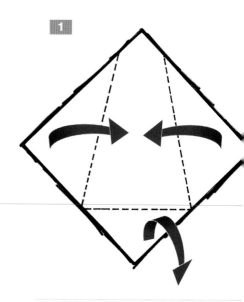

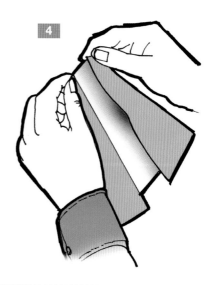

2

3

5

TOPIARY DOGS

For all those dog lovers who also enjoy gardening and the pleasures of horticulture, what could be more rewarding than creating a piece of living art in the form of a topiary dog? Traditionally, topiary figures have been created by lovingly clipping a slow-growing shrub or hedging plant, such as box or yew, into the desired shape. It looks great but it takes years to achieve! But the good news is that, if you want faster results, there is another way that takes some of the waiting out of wanting.

Choice of frame

Today, it is possible to buy ready-made wire frames from special manufacturers or from garden centers that relieve the prospective topiarist of the task of constructing the underlying frame. They are available in a wide variety of animal shapes including a number of appealing dogs. But inevitably, you are restricted by the patterns that are commercially available. For those who really want to let their imaginations run riot, it is relatively straightforward to create a frame from sturdy wire that can be covered with netting and used as the structure over which plants can be trained to grow. This lovable flower-bearing dog is just one example of what can be achieved by using this technique.

1 The flower basket that our topiary dog bears in his mouth is lined with a hanging-basket liner, filled with soil and planted seasonally.

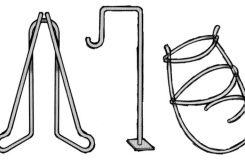

Planting designs

For this method the frame is covered with wire netting and fast-growing ivy plants are encouraged to grow up out of a container and over the form. The stems can be wired securely to the frame and the whole living sculpture clipped to shape as it grows. The floral basket adds a nice splash of seasonal color to complete the effect.

4 Along with the head, the dog is made of separate sections that comprise the body, front legs, rear legs/base, and a hook on which the flower basket hangs.

2 The base is a sturdy lined container of soil into which the fast-growing vine or ivy plants are rooted.

3 The frame is made from several individual components that are wired together. Here we see how the head is made up of several individual lengths of strong garden wire that are bent and curved into shape and then bound together tightly.

Narrow gauge wire is flexible and binds the joints.

Wire netting covers the framework.

5 The finished frame is positioned on the container and plants are trained to grow over it. They are wired in place and neatly clipped to shape. An extra splash of color is provided by using blooms to represent the eyes.

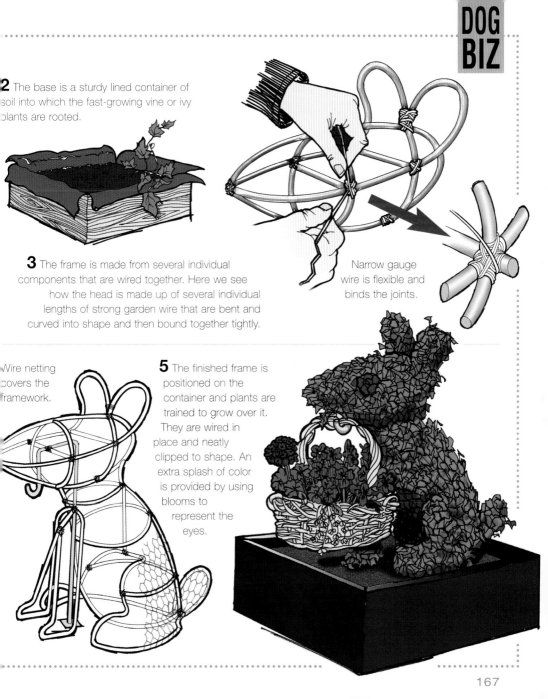

A PAPIER-MÂCHÉ DOG

You will need:
Empty plastic bottle
Thin stick or cane
Bubble wrap
Wallpaper paste
Newspaper
Non-shiny adhesive tape

1 Scrunch bubble wrap into a roughly triangular shape and tape it to the weighted bottle.

2 Screw up bubble wrap into a ball and then add a slightly elongated muzzle section and two floppy ears. Secure the head section tightly with adhesive tape and sit it firmly on a stick that you have mounted in the bottle.

3 Tear newspaper into narrow strips. One at a time, apply paste to the paper and cover the basic shape with overlapping strips, laying alternate layers horizontally and vertically.

4 On the front of the body section, add rolls of bubble wrap to build up the shape of forelegs and front paws. Then cover the legs and paws with more strips of paper to create a smooth finish. Use a thin roll of bubble wrap to form a tail, and attach this to the body with more paper strips.

5 Your model should now look like this. Allow it to dry for a week or so before painting it.

6 After the paint has dried, use a magic marker pen to add details such as eyes, nose, mouth, and whiskers.

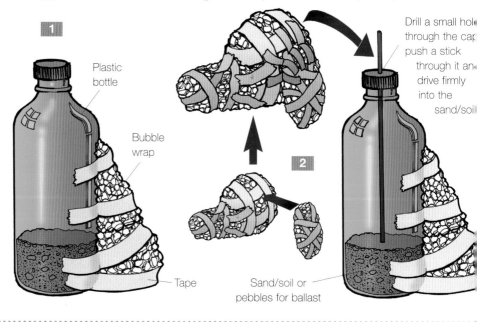

Plastic bottle

Bubble wrap

Drill a small hole through the cap, push a stick through it and drive firmly into the sand/soil

Tape

Sand/soil or pebbles for ballast

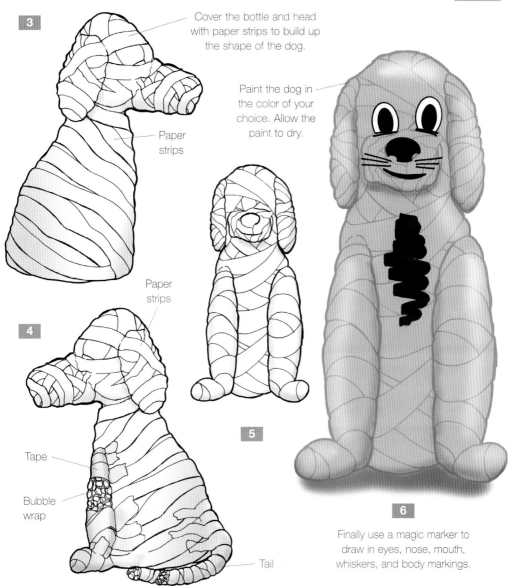

3

Cover the bottle and head with paper strips to build up the shape of the dog.

Paint the dog in the color of your choice. Allow the paint to dry.

Paper strips

Paper strips

4

Tape

Bubble wrap

5

Tail

6

Finally use a magic marker to draw in eyes, nose, mouth, whiskers, and body markings.

DOG CARE

Vaccination

Vaccination against common killer diseases such as distemper, leptospirosis, and parvorvirus is essential, along with regular boosters. Dogs can catch these killer diseases not only directly from other dogs, but by sniffing where other dogs have been or even from humans unwittingly carrying infection between canines, so play safe. Worming and flea treatment also need to be carried out regularly.

Neutering

You don't have to have your dog neutered, but if you don't, it is your responsibility to prevent the birth of unwanted puppies. Male dogs should never be allowed to roam, and females need to be segregated when in season, usually twice a year. Neutering prevents gynecological ailments to which unspayed bitches are prone. It isn't a cure-all for behavioral problems, but can help with those that are hormone-based.

Safety first

Don't let curiosity kill your puppy! Dog-proofing your home can save your pet's life. Put away household chemicals such as detergents and bleach, along with medicines and small objects such as rubber bands and paperclips that can

HEALTH – COMMON WARNING SIGNS

SYMPTOMS	COMMON CAUSES	ACTION
Scratching, excess licking	Parasites; allergies; wounds	Check skin for flea droppings (apply flea spray) or wounds (may need veterinary attention).
Shaking head and scratching ears	Ear mites; ear infection	Check ears for dark, gritty wax (apply mite medication) or inflammation (see veterinarian—never neglect infections).
Bad breath and drooling	Gum infection/ tooth problems	See veterinarian. Reduce risk in future by cleaning teeth with doggy toothpaste (right).
Runny nose and sneezing	Viral or bacterial infection; allergy; foreign body in nose	See veterinarian. Prevent infections by vaccination. Allergies may respond to treatment. Foreign bodies not uncommon.
Runny or inflamed eyes	Viral or bacterial infection; injury	See veterinarian. Prevent infections by vaccination. Never neglect eye injuries.

To you it's rubbish, to your ▶▶
dog, it's a delicatessen! Bins
need to be securely dog-proof.

be swallowed. Watch out
for hazardous waste (most
dogs can raid waste
bins), electrical wires that
could be chewed, and
open upstairs windows
that your pet might jump
through.

Paw maintenance

Keep paws clean! Dogs don't have shoes to
protect their feet, so check paws after walks for
sharp objects such as grass seeds that can

work their way in and sticky stuff
such as chewing gum, which can damage
the skin. Toenails need regular inspection; if they
don't get enough wear to keep them short, they
will need clipping to prevent them from growing
into the pads—and don't forget the dewclaws!

⬆ *Accustom your dog to having his nails checked
and clipped while he is still a puppy, or you
may have problems restraining him as an adult.*

THE DOG IN OLD AGE

How old is old?

It used to be said that one year of a dog's life equaled seven years of a human life, but the equation doesn't work out so neatly. For one thing, large breeds tend to age earlier and have shorter lifespans than smaller ones. Overall, the average canine lifespan is about 13 years; but for the Bernese Mountain Dog, for example, some surveys suggest a lifespan as short as 6-8 years, while many Chihuahuas reach the age of 20 years.

⤒ Old dogs need extra care, such as extra grooming and attention to diet, as well as frequent check-ups for the first signs of any developing physical problems.

Oldest dog

An increasing number of dogs are living into their late twenties, although none has yet broken the 30-year barrier. The oldest documented dog was Bluey, an Australian Cattle Dog that attained 29 years and 5 months. Britain's oldest dog was a Papillon named Fred, who won the Special Veteran Stakes at Crufts when he was a mere 20 years old and went on to reach the age of 29 years.

Signs of aging

Dogs age in the same way as people. They are likely to develop

◀◀ When an old dog finds it hard to get in and out of the car, a ramp saves his dignity—and spares his owner from having to lift him.

stiff joints, weaker digestive systems, and reduced energy levels. Their fur may become thinner, and they feel the cold more. Hearing and sight may deteriorate, sleeping patterns alter, and there may be behavioral changes such as irritability, disorientation, or lapses in house-training, which require considerable treatment.

Failing senses

Sight and hearing often deteriorate in older dogs, but most cope well with disability, depending increasingly on their remaining senses, particularly smell, to compensate. Deaf dogs may wander off on walks; they can't hear the recall, so keep an eye on them. Blind dogs usually adjust extremely well, and you can help by not moving furniture so that they know the lay-out of each room.

Do dogs get Alzheimer's disease?

Senile confusion in dogs is not termed Alzheimer's disease, but some old dogs do display disorientation, forgetfulness, and behavioral changes along the same lines as Alzheimer's sufferers. Veterinarians call the condition "canine cognitive dysfunction," and can prescribe medication that seems to help in some cases.

CARE OF THE ELDERLY DOG: TOP TIPS

1. Exercise	It's important to keep an old dog active, but several short walks are better than one long one.
2. Diet	Watch out for increase or loss of weight, and adjust food quantities accordingly. Several small meals per day suit an aging digestive system better than one big one.
3. Grooming	Extra grooming maintains hygiene, improves circulation, and eases stiffness. Nails may need cutting more frequently.
4. Sleeping	Old dogs sleep more and need a comfortable bed. Sleep patterns often change, with more daytime dozes and more restless nights.
5. Stimulus	Don't let your old dog become a vegetable. Mental stimulation will help him stay alert and enjoy life.
6. Health	Slowing down, incontinence, or irritability in the old dog may not be due to the effects of age but to illness. Let your veterinarian decide the cause. Regular medical checkups make sense.

Boosting brainpower

A dog's brain slows down with age; literally. In youth, his nervous system transmits messages at a rate of some 20,000 feet (6,000 m) per second, but in old age this drops to about 4,250 feet (1,300 m) per second. Most dogs over 16 years show signs of reduced brain function. However, keeping your dog's mind busy can delay this process; mental stimulation helps to improve the function of brain cells, so keep up training.

Old dog, new tricks

It's never too late to learn. Pockets, an Australian Shepherd, was a veteran with serious health problems when Massachusetts Aussie Rescue retrieved her from a lonely life in a concrete run. This unpromising start didn't deter new owner Adam Conn from training her for rally work (a mix of obedience and agility), and in 2005, at the age of 15 years, she became the oldest dog ever to earn an American Kennel Club title.

HOROSCOPES

Aries
(March 21st–April 20th)
Dogs born under the sign of Aries are fun companions rather than restful pets—bold, energetic, and adventurous. Their high energy levels and need for occupation make them ideal candidates for challenging activities such as field trials or flyball. The Aries dog can be intolerant of other canines; he needs good socialization in puppyhood to teach him manners, or he may grow up to be something of a bully.

Taurus
(April 21st–May 21st)
The Taurean dog has a happy, easygoing personality. He likes his comforts, and owners need to provide him with enough physical and mental exercise to prevent him from becoming a couch potato. Although he can be lazy, he has a good brain when pushed into using it, and can be trained to a high standard. He enjoys his food a bit too much, and can become overweight if attention is not paid to his diet.

Gemini *(May 22nd–June 21st)*
Gemini dogs are always puppies at heart. Lively, fidgety, and often restless, they like to be at the

center of the action. They demand attention and will often get into mischief simply to make you take notice of them. They can be a real challenge to train, as they are easily bored, but if you can keep your Gemini dog's interest, this natural show-off will impress you with his quickness to learn.

Cancer
(June 22nd–July 22nd)
The Cancerian dog is one of the most sensitive of all the zodiac signs. He is easily upset by disruptions to his routine, changes of diet, or emotional scenes among his human family, and needs plenty of calm, sensible reassurance. A sympathetic companion for an equally sensitive owner, he may become neurotic in a noisy and chaotic household. He enjoys his walks, and will often benefit from swimming.

Leo *(July 23rd–August 22nd)*
The Leo dog is, in his own opinion at least, the King (or Queen) of Beasts and wants to be the center of attention. He is usually outgoing and gregarious, expecting people to enjoy his company as much as he does theirs. However,

his dignity matters to him, and he is easily offended if not treated with respect. In a multi-dog household he expects to be top dog, but is a benevolent ruler rather than a bully.

Virgo *(August 23rd– September 23rd)*

The Virgo dog is a fastidious, even fussy, creature that likes to have things just so and appreciates a regular routine. His taste for order often makes him a great working dog that gets satisfaction from carrying out his tasks to perfection. In a rowdy, disorderly household his virtues will often go overlooked and he may become shy and withdrawn. He can be picky over food and needs care over his diet.

Libra *(September 24th– October 23rd)*

Libran dogs are sociable creatures that need plenty of company, are unsuited to being left alone by

Since ancient times, man has believed that the cyclical movement of planets affects our lives and behavior—and those of our pets.

working owners, and are often happiest in a multidog household. They enjoy outings and visitors, and adapt well to changes in circumstances. They like to have their own way, but tend to achieve this by persuasion rather than outright demands, and owners may not realize how skillfully they are being manipulated.

Scorpio *(October 24th– November 22nd)*

Scorpio dogs can be demanding pets. Strong-willed, highly focused, and active, they put everything they have into whatever they are doing at the moment, whether that be playing, demanding food, cuddling, or sleeping. The Scorpio dog never forgets a friend or an enemy. He is devoted to his owners, but not necessarily obedient, especially if something else is engaging his interest at the time.

HOROSCOPES *(CONTINUED)*

Sagittarius
(November 23rd–
December 21st)

The Sagittarius dog is a whirlwind of energy. Confident, energetic, and fond of his own way, he loves to explore and makes a great companion for those who enjoy long country walks, though owners will have to work on his recall! Capturing and maintaining his interest can be a challenge, as he is easily distracted, but persuade him that lessons are fun and he will astonish you with his quickness to learn.

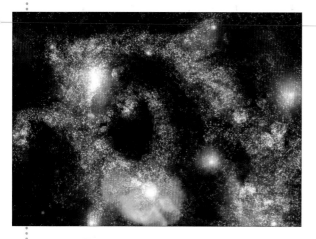

⬆ *The star signs of Western astrology bear little relation to the constellations they are named for.*

Capricorn
(December 22nd–
January 20th)

Patient and persistent, the Capricorn dog probably inspired the word "dogged." Once he has an idea in mind, he won't let it go. This can make him a great worker, but may also mean that he will finish

what he is doing before he listens to you calling. He likes his home comforts, he likes routine, and he is quietly but unchangeably devoted to his owner—but that doesn't mean he has to be obedient!

Aquarius
(January 21st–
February 19th)

The Aquarius dog is a unique individual, quirky, unpredictable, and full of personality. Intelligent, intuitive, often highly inventive, he is an entertaining companion that can be a real clown and loves to show off how clever he is. He is a quick learner, but not the choice for those who want regimented obedience. Routine exercises bore him, and he prefers to invent his own variations.

Pisces *(February 20th–*
March 20th)

Pisces is the sign of the dreamer, and it may be hard to work out just where your Pisces dog's mind is wandering. This is a dog that needs a peaceful home with some quiet time to himself (which is not to say he likes being ignored). Highly sensitive to those they live with, Piscean dogs often seem to have extrasensory perception, coming before they are called and knowing when their owners are coming home unexpectedly.

Christmas puppies

The worst sign for a puppy to be born under may be Scorpio, for that makes him just the right age to become a Christmas gift. Dog-lovers know that "A dog is for life, not just for Christmas," but every year dog shelters fill up with castoffs. For this reason, most reputable

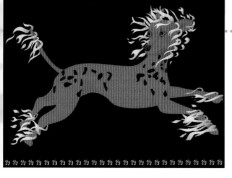

Model dogs and traditional paper designs adorn Chinese homes in the Year of the Dog.

breeders won't sell puppies at this time of year, and caring buyers will be prepared to wait until the festive season is over.

Eastern horoscopes

The Chinese zodiac runs through a cycle of 12 lunar years, each having the sign of an animal: Rat, Ox, Tiger, Rabbit (or Cat), Dragon, Snake, Horse, Sheep, Monkey, Rooster, Dog, and Pig. Legend says that Buddha invited all the animals of the world to a feast, but only these 12 arrived. They were rewarded by each having a year named after them, in the order of their arrival.

⩡ *The symbols for the 12 animals of the Chinese lunar years. The Dog symbol is the third sign from the left on the bottom row.*

牛龙马羊兔蛇

The Year of the Dog

Beginning	Ending	Beginning	Ending
February 10th, 1910	January 29th, 1911	February 6th, 1970	January 26th, 1971
January 28th, 1922	February 15th, 1923	January 25th, 1982	February 12th, 1983
February 14th, 1934	February 3rd, 1935	February 10th, 1994	January 30th, 1995
February 2nd, 1946	January 21st, 1947	January 29th, 2006	February 17th, 2007
February 18th, 1958	February 7th, 1959	February 16th, 2018	February 4th, 2019

People born in the Year of the Dog are said to be honest, loyal, and generous, though stubborn and also prone to worrying. They make great teachers, social workers, lawyers, and activists.

猪鼠狗虎猴鸡

DOG TRAINING

Why train your dog?

Dogs don't **need** obedience training, so long as they receive "convenience training" in the form of basic good manners. However, taking training further via obedience, agility, or any other route provides mental stimulation to make your dog's life more interesting and prevent him from growing old and stodgy before his time. It shouldn't be about boring, repetitive exercises, but about dog and owner having fun together.

◄◄ *Agility training provides physical and mental exercise to help keep your dog fit.*

Force training

In the bad old days, most dog trainers used forcible means; in fact, they spoke of "dog breaking" rather than training. Today, a wide range of gentler approaches is available, and there should be no place for rough handling. "Force training" now should mean no more than putting a dog into the desired position; for example, pressing lightly on a puppy's rear end to push him into the *"Sit,"* rather than simply encouraging him verbally.

Pack rules and dominance

Many dog training theories are founded on the idea of a strict hierarchy of dominance supposedly based on the natural rules of a wolf pack, to ensure that the dog knows he is of lower status than his human family. This is a human rather than a canine concept! It discourages novices from treating dogs like little humans, but it can lead to rigid rules and misunderstandings between dog and owner.

Start right

It was once thought that training should not start until a puppy was six months old, but it's never too early to begin. When a puppy is aged about 7–14 weeks, it passes through a period of rapid learning that should not be wasted. In fact, puppies start learning how to interact with people even before they leave their mothers, so proper early socialization is the best foundation for training.

Lead training is easiest if you start before ▲ your puppy is old enough to go for walks.

Letting it happen

Puppies learn most quickly if you make use of their natural actions. For example, you can teach *"Sit"* by holding a treat just above the head *(right),* when the puppy will naturally plonk his bottom down to reach up. As he does so, give the command,

and then reward him. He will quickly learn to associate word and action.

Reward and punishment

Dogs respond best to reward-based teaching methods, whether you use treats, praise, or hugging. The most effective punishment is to make undesirable actions unrewarding by ignoring them. A puppy soon learns that you stop play when he nips, turn away when he jumps up, etc. Where bad behavior cannot be ignored, prevention is better than cure (such as keeping your dog on leash among livestock to prevent sheep-chasing).

Clicker training

Clicker training is a very effective reward-based system. The trainer uses the sound of a clicker to identify a desired action, following this up with a reward (usually a food treat). The dog soon learns that the clicker sound means "Yes, that's what I want—and there's a reward coming." Once he is eager to repeat the action for you, the verbal cue (*"Sit," "Down,"* etc.) can be added.

Trainable breeds

Stanley Coren, a dog trainer and professor of psychology, carried out a survey comparing the trainability of 133 different breeds. Border

◀◀ Food rewards will motivate most dogs to learn, though some work better for praise, cuddling or a game with a special toy.

Collies, Poodles, and German Shepherds came first on his list; Bulldogs, Basenjis, and Afghan Hounds at the bottom. At the same time, however, he pointed out that much hinges on the trainer. A good trainer can achieve excellent results with a supposedly difficult breed.

▼ Border Collies top the list for trainability, but their brains, energy, and working drive may actually make them less easy to train for the novice than more laid-back breeds.

ACTIVITIES WITH YOUR DOG

Obedience work

Joining a local obedience club can be a great way of building up your relationship with your dog. A dog's mind needs exercise just as much as his body, and a few minutes' training every day can be very rewarding for both of you.

Obedience trials, which test the ability of owner and dog to work together as a team, are not just for the experts but are scheduled at various levels from beginners on up.

◀◀ *Teaching your dog to sit on command is no formality; it could save his life if he is running off in traffic.*

Working trials

For owners of working breeds, working trials may be more fun than competitive obedience. This sport requires dogs to demonstrate their skill in three elements: nosework (tracking and searching), control (obedience to basic commands), and agility (long jump and scaling a high jump). Originally designed to test working ability, it offers both physical and mental exercise for dogs and their owners.

Field trials

Gundogs have their own competitive sport in the form of field trials, which test their working ability in a scenario set up to resemble, as closely as possible, a day's shooting in the field. This is a hobby for owners who love to see dogs working in their traditional role, and for dogs bred from working stock; many show strains have lost much of their hunting drive.

▲ *Sharing outdoor activities with your dog helps to build up a close relationship, as well as providing mental and physical stimulation.*

Schutzhund

Schutzhund ("protection dog") work was developed in Germany in the early 1900s specifically to test the working skills of German Shepherd Dogs, though it is open to any guard breed. Dogs are tested in tracking, obedience, and protection work. This is a specialized and demanding test, and few dogs that have not been bred for Schutzhund will pass it.

↥ *Russ Williams, who teaches martial arts in North Wales, has taught his Russian Black Terrier, Ringo Tsar, the art of kickboxing.*

The show circuit

Dog shows are "beauty contests" for the various breeds, but there is a great deal more to them than buying a well-bred puppy and entering it in a show. Show dogs need to learn how to behave in the ring to show themselves to best advantage, and owners need to learn handling and presentation skills. Showing dogs is an absorbing, if often expensive hobby, sometimes at the expense of the dogs concerned, if winning becomes more important than having fun with your canine friend.

Flyball

Another energetic sport, flyball is a team game in which relay teams of dogs race against each other over hurdles toward a box where they press a spring-loaded pad to release a tennis ball, catch the ball, and dash back with it to the start. Invented in California in the 1970s, flyball quickly caught on and is now popular worldwide. It's an ideal sport for dogs that enjoy ball games.

Agility

Growing in popularity, agility is an exhilarating sport *(below)* for energetic dogs and energetic owners. Dogs are required to race through an obstacle course, and are marked on both speed and accuracy. They run off leash, guided only by voice commands, so they need to be well trained and attentive to their owners. Fast, enthusiastic breeds such as Border Collies and Australian Shepherds are popular, but most dogs can enjoy agility.

Dancing with dogs

If you love music and you love dog training, dancing with your dog is a great way to combine the two. This increasingly popular hobby started out as "heelwork to music," but has developed into "freestyle" dancing, a spectacular showcase for dogs' ability to work with their owners. A growing number of obedience clubs are offering dancing classes. If there is one in your area, why not give it a try?

MORE ACTIVITIES WITH YOUR DOG

Sheepdog trials

A surprising number of town-dwelling Border Collie addicts spend their weekends on farms training their dogs to make the most of their inherited instincts. Nobody wants these superb workers to dwindle into mere show dogs, and sheepdog trials enable them to display their skill at moving sheep around a field, through gates, and into enclosures as directed by their handlers.

⬆ *Border Collies and Working Sheepdogs are the breeds of choice for sheepdog trials, but other breeds such as Corgis also hold herding trials.*

Tracking

You may prefer training your dog to track a scent, either as a hobby that both of you can enjoy or as a competitive sport in which you can enter tracking trials. Both dog and owner need to be in good physical condition, for tracking involves a great deal of walking, often over rough terrain. You will also need access to land where you can lay tracks for your dog to follow.

⬆ *It takes a fair commitment of time and money to keep sled dogs in good racing condition.*

Sledding

Husky owners don't need to let an absence of snow stop them from enjoying dog sledding. The development of wheeled rigs has made sled dog racing a hobby that can be enjoyed on grass or forest tracks. You don't even need a traditional sled dog breed. In the 1980s, John Suter ran a team of Standard Poodles in the grueling Iditarod race, while today, one of Britain's top sled dogs is Buster, a German Short-haired Pointer,

Cross-country racing

Cani-cross combines walking the dog with marathon training, in a cross-country race that's

ideal for dogs and owners who love to run. Originally a means of keeping sled dogs fit between races, it has become a sport in its own right. Runners wear a belt to which the dog's harness is attached by a lead with an elasticized attachment, and are towed along by dog power.

⌃ *Hannah the Newfoundland provides wheeled transport for arthritic Labrador Oliver.*

Carting

Today, dogs pull carts for fun more often than for work. Traditional draft breeds such as Newfoundlands are most commonly seen, but even toy breeds can pull miniature carts. Various styles of harness, carts and wagons are available, most spectacular being the traditional decorated milk carts for Bernese Mountain

Dogs. Carting clubs, where you can learn to train your dog, are springing up everywhere as the sport grows in popularity.

Pet therapy

If you have a friendly, well-behaved dog that loves visiting people, he might be a candidate for pet therapy work, visiting hospitals and senior citizen's homes to provide mental and physical stimulation. Various organizations exist to encourage volunteers to carry out this valuable work. Therapy dogs cheer up patients, and can often make contact with those who have withdrawn from human communication.

Search and rescue

Locating lost walkers and disaster victims, the task of search and rescue dogs, is a task that requires dedication, yet most of the work is done by volunteers. Dogs and handlers participate in lengthy training sessions before they set out to work in the field. This is a hobby that saves lives, if you have the commitment, physical fitness, and a suitable dog (typically a medium-sized working breed).

◄◄ *Most dogs just love to run, but the number of places where they can run free are sadly reduced nowadays.*

⌃ *Mountain rescue and avalanche dogs undergo meticulous training, and have to be ready for work whenever the call goes out.*

DOGS BEHAVING BADLY (and how to cope)

Jumping up

It may be cute when a puppy jumps up to say hello, but it's not so appealing when you're faced with a grown dog with muddy feet. You can avoid problems by teaching your dog to sit when he comes to greet you, so that you can make a fuss over him in comfort. This is especially important with big dogs that can easily bowl over a child or frail elderly person with an overenthusiastic greeting.

If you enjoy your dog doing ▸▸ this, still teach him to jump up only when invited, to avoid accidents.

Chewing

Puppies chew when they are teething, and it is essential to direct them to approved chew toys rather than your belongings. Adult dogs can also be destructive, often when they are stressed, lonely, or understimulated. More exercise may help your dog to relax and doze when left, or you can provide a food-stuffed toy for hours of entertainment. Spreading unpleasant-tasting substances on the furniture rarely works!

Pulling on the leash

Dogs that pull on the leash are no fun to walk, and risk damage to their necks and throats. Prevention is less trouble

HOUSE-TRAINING PROBLEMS
Establish the cause before working on the cure.

Overly timid dogs	Submissive urination, especially when greeting people, is meant as an appeasement gesture. Such dogs need their confidence built up, not scolding.
Males	Territorial marking may be down to bumptious masculinity or to stress. Castration is rarely a cure once the habit is formed; intensive supervision and retraining is needed.
Confusion	Too much scolding can muddle a puppy into thinking it safer to mess out of sight behind the sofa than in full view in the garden. Put more emphasis on encouraging good behavior than rebuking bad!
Stress	Loneliness, boredom, insecurity, and separation anxiety can lead to problems.
Lack of access to outdoors	Play fair—don't shut a dog indoors for long periods and expect him to hang on! Make sure he has frequent opportunities for outdoor toileting.
Physical illness	Lapses in house-training may have a physical cause; if in doubt, book a veterinary checkup.

than a cure; don't let puppies get away with behavior that will be a nuisance when they grow up. A slow but effective cure is to stop whenever your dog pulls, moving on only when the leash is slack. Many confirmed pullers respond well to a headcollar, which gives the owner more control.

Recall problems

Many owners actually teach their dogs not to come when called, by only calling their pet at the end of a walk when the fun is over. They then make things worse by scolding the dog for not coming at once. It's important to make the recall rewarding. Practice by calling your dog to you three or four times on every walk, giving him a treat or a hug when he comes and then letting him run off again.

⬆ *Rewarding good behavior with a treat or fuss helps to discourage bad behavior.*

Digging

A confirmed digger can ruin a garden in a very short time. Leaving a puppy unsupervised in the garden with nothing in particular to do is inviting trouble. He will learn that he isn't supposed to dig only if you are out there with him to make it clear. Some dogs dig because they are bored, and providing more activities will help. Others are digging addicts, and it may be best to provide them with a dedicated area of their own.

⬆ *Encouraging him to play with your laces now is a sure route to chewed shoes later on.*

Nipping and mouthing

Puppies don't have hands, so they use their mouths to play and investigate the world. They don't know that it hurts when they nip human hands, so it's important to teach them by halting play instantly when they do so. Excited mouthing in play is best discouraged, but some dogs (gundog breeds in particular) like to take a hand gently in their mouths as a gesture of affection.

THE NAMING OF DOGS

Name sources

More than half of us give our dogs human names such as Sam or Suzie. Dog names are also often based on the dog's appearance (Spot or Blackie) or character (Nip or Bouncer), or on things we like (Candy, Whiskey, or Blossom). Today, celebrities provide an increasingly popular source of names: a recent survey came up with Rambo, Rocky, Ozzy, Elvis, Posh, and Britney as new favorites.

⬆ Are they fighting, or playing? Research showed that people interpreted dogs' behavior differently when the dogs were given friendly or aggressive-sounding names.

Top Five Tips on Naming Your Dog
1 Short names are easiest for dogs to learn and owners to use.
2 Names that sound like common commands may cause confusion (Noah sounds like *"No"*).
3 Before you settle on a name, imagine yourself shouting it in the park.
4 Overpopular names can cause confusion if you call your dog in a park full of dogs with the same name.
5 Think ahead. Jokes grow stale, fashions change, puppies grow up—pick a name you'll still like in ten years' time!

Give a dog a bad name

People judge a dog by his name, so a dog named Bruiser or Rocky is less likely to win friends than one named Pal or Buddy. One behaviorist asked people to watch a video of a dog jumping up at a man. When he called the dog Ripper, Slasher, or other "tough" names, most viewers saw the dog's behavior as hostile, but when he gave him a positive name such as Happy, most viewers saw it as friendly and playful.

Traditional names

Among pet dogs, old-fashioned names such as Fido and Rover have disappeared. But many working sheepdogs still answer to the traditional names of their ancestors, such as Nell, Cap, Glen, Moss, Mist, Hemp, Tweed, and Clyde. English hound packs also preserve old names, including those recommended by Greek writer Xenophon (430–354 B.C.), such as Psyche and Hybris.

Kennel names

Most pedigree dogs have two names—one official and one for everyday use. For example, the 2005 Crufts Best In Show winner is officially named "Cracknor Cause Célèbre," but she answers to "Coco." The official name registered with a national Kennel Club is unique to each dog, always starts with the name of the

TOP TEN MOST POPULAR NAMES

	U.K. Male	U.K. Female	U.S.A. Male	U.S.A. Female
1	Sam	Trixie	Max	Maggie
2	Spot	Polly	Jake	Molly
3	Pip	Jessie	Buddy	Lady
4	Duke	Lucy	Bailey	Sadie
5	Piper	Bonnie	Sam	Lucy
6	Max	Cassie	Rocky	Daisy
7	Charlie	Daisy	Buster	Ginger
8	Rocky	Heidi	Casey	Abby
9	Zak	Susie	Cody	Sasha
10	Tiny	Holly	Duke	Sandy

"Mind Your Own Business" or "My Neighbor Is Ungrateful." Calling the dog by its name in public lets the owner express views and feelings without having to address members of the community directly. Conveniently, names such as "Whatever You Do, People Will Gossip About You" are shorter in the local language.

...or making them worse

This approach worked less well for a Hong Kong man who had a long-standing feud with the woman next door. He bought himself a dog that he named Ling Ling after his neighbor, and proceeded to curse it loudly in public, shouting its name throughout. However, all this achieved was a law-suit against him for damaging his neighbor's reputation.

▲ *2004 Crufts winner Ch. Cobyco Call the Tune answers to "Dee Dee."*

breeder's kennel (here "Cracknor"), and is rarely known to the dog itself!

Smoothing social problems...

In Ghana, people use dogs' names to tackle social problems. Dogs are given names such as

NAMES THAT LIVE ON

The taxman's dog

Louis Dobermann (1823–1894), a German magistrate, designed his own breed of guard dog to assist him on his tax-collecting rounds. No one knows quite what breeds and strains he used—the fact that he was also the local dogcatcher probably played a part in his breeding program. He lived to see the breed achieve official recognition in Germany in 1900, and today, the Doberman Pinscher is one of the most popular working breeds.

▲ *Louis Dobermann's breed has been much refined—his dogs were almost of Rottweiler type.*

Coonhound creators

In the United States, Jonathan Plott of North Carolina, Peter Redbone of Tennessee, and Thomas Walker of Virginia all gave their names to breeds of Coonhound. The Plott Hound, bred by the Plott family from hounds they brought with them from Germany in the 1750s, is said to be of almost pure German stock, but the Treeing Walker and Redbone Coonhounds share English Foxhound ancestry.

Scandinavian hounds

Four 19th-century Scandinavian breeders immortalized their names in new hound breeds, blending local

◄◄ *The Dunker descends from local scenthounds crossed with Russian Harlequin Hounds.*

▲ *The Hamiltonstövare's ancestry includes several German and English hound breeds.*

strains with imported dogs from Germany, England, and even Russia. Wilhelm Dunker created the Dunker, Per Schiller the Schillerstövare, Per Hygen the Hygenhund, and Adolf Patrick Hamilton (founder of the Swedish Kennel Club) the Hamiltonstövare, the only one known outside Scandinavia today.

The parson's terriers

The Jack Russell Terrier is among the best-loved breeds today. But its originator, hunting parson John Russell (1795–1883), never set out to found a breed, merely to establish a kennel of the best type of Fox Terrier. As Fox Terriers turned into smart show dogs, Russell's name remained attached to working strains, and today denotes two distinct breeds—the long-legged Parson Russell and short-legged Jack Russell.

A modern ratter

In the 1960s, eccentric hunter, author, and canine geneticist David Brian Plummer set out to create "the supreme rat hunting dog" from a mix of Beagle, Bull Terrier, Fell Terrier, and Jack Russell. Today, the handsome copper and white Plummer Terrier is well known among hunting men, although Kennel Club recognition has not as yet been sought.

Fictional Farmer

The Dandie Dinmont Terrier is the only breed named for a fictional character. Until the early 19th century, it was just another local strain of terrier known as the "mustard and pepper" from its tan and gray colors. But when Sir Walter Scott, in his 1815 novel *Guy Mannering*, created the farmer Dandie Dinmont with his mustard and pepper terriers, the public's fancy was captured—and the breed acquired a name.

A ducal setter

The handsome black and tan Gordon Setter owes its name to Alexander, fourth Duke of Gordon (1743–1827), who established a famous strain at Gordon Castle, Scotland, some say by introducing a dash of Collie blood to his setters. Like many breed founders, he might be surprised by the modern edition, in which the white markings common to most of his dogs are outlawed.

▲ *The Gordon Setter is the only gundog to be numbered among Scotland's native breeds.*

A king and a politician

King Charles II *(above top)* is unique in having not one, but two breeds named for him, although the King Charles and Cavalier King Charles Spaniels *(above)* are both offshoots of the same royal lapdogs. Also linked with a public figure is the Keeshond, named for Cornelius ("Kees") de Gyselaer, a noted patriot of the 18th century in Holland, who kept one as his constant companion and made the breed the mascot of the Patriots' Party.

PUBS AND DOGS

A drink with the dog

Since 1393, when King Richard II ordered that all public houses and inns had to display a sign, British pub signs have played host to a wide variety of ingenious names. One recent survey came up with the figure of 19,500 different pub names, and dogs feature in a great many, producing some very attractive and interesting signs.

The Greyhound

A very common pub name, this often indicates an heraldic figure on the coat of arms of a local dignitary. Reflecting the days of horse-drawn

☙ *An unusual wall-mounted sign dated 1703 at the Greyhound Inn, Shap, Cumbria, England.*

coaches, some allude to the silver greyhound badge worn until the late 18th century by King's Messengers who carried state mail, while others were named after a fast mailcoach service—like modern Greyhound buses.

A great Greyhound

Other Greyhound pubs honor actual racing or coursing dogs, such as The Nettle (Milltown, Derbyshire). Originally The Greyhound, the pub was renamed by a long-ago landlord after his own Greyhound, first simply as The Nettle, then, to celebrate the dog's success in a premier race, The Well Run Nettle. The name has changed twice since then, reverting to The Nettle in 1998.

Dressed-up Dogs

A popular pub name, the Dog in a Doublet may refer to the protective coat, or doublet, worn by hunting boarhounds, the bright identifying jackets worn by wildfowlers'

Sign painters have had a lot of fun with the ☙ "Dog in a Doublet" theme. This comical little fellow looks like one of the performing dogs popular in Victorian times.

dogs, or the gaudy costumes of the performing dogs of traveling showmen. The Dog and Muffler, at Coleford, Gloucester, however, takes its name from the local miners' custom of tying up their dogs with their mufflers while they drank.

⬆ *Another humorous sign shows the sly fox watching as the dog follows the wrong trail.*

Hunting dogs

Pub signs celebrating hunting with dogs abound—the Dog and Gun, Dog and Duck, Dog and Fox, Dog and Otter, Dog and Partridge, Fox and Hounds, Hare and Hounds, etc. Individual hounds may be commemorated, as at the Hark to Bounty (Slaidburn,

Lancashire), which acquired its name in 1875 when the local squire's drinking was interrupted by Bounty, his favorite hound, baying outside.

A fake legend

In 1793, the landlord of the Royal Goat Hotel at Bedd Gelert, South Wales, brought it fame with a name change. Bedd Gelert translates as "the grave of Gelert," so he invented the tale of Gelert the Greyhound, whose master killed him when he saw the bloodstained dog by his child's cradle, realizing too late Gelert had killed a wolf to protect the baby. Tourists to this day visit Gelert's supposed grave, and the nearby hostelry.

The Black Dog

A ghost story lies behind the name of the Black Dog Inn near Uplyme, Devon. The tale goes that in the 18th century a ghostly black dog kept appearing at the fireside of a local farmer, and eventually led him to a cache of gold coins hidden in his attic. The farmer used these to buy the inn, which he named after the helpful phantom. The dog is still said to haunt a nearby road, now named Dog Lane.

Not what it seems

The Dog and Bacon in Horsham, Sussex, displays a sign *(right)* with a handsome Border Collie making off with a bacon joint, suggesting a tale of a hound stealing some-

one's breakfast that will ring bells with many dog owners. However, the name is said to be in fact a corruption of "Dorking Beacon," a nearby hill that can be seen from the pub on a clear day.

CATS, HORSES, AND OTHER FRIENDS

aggressive cats will swipe a dog's nose instead of running away, which doesn't help the situation. However, cats and dogs that live together are often the best of friends.

Cats' best friend

Between 1990 and 2005 an American dog named Ginny became famous as "the dog who loved cats." Starting by rescuing a litter of kittens trapped in a pipe, she went on to save more than 900 endangered felines, even digging through broken glass to find an injured cat. In 1998, her dedication earned her the title of Westchester Feline Club Cat of the Year [sic], and her memorial service in 2005 was attended by 300 cats.

⏫ *Puppies and kittens make friends readily, but kittens' sharp claws can do unintentional damage so play should always be supervised.*

Stable companions

Dogs and horses have gone together throughout history. Packhounds bred to work with mounted hunters developed a real affinity with horses, as did carriage dogs trained to run alongside horse-drawn coaches, initially as guards and later as smart status symbols. Dogs were often kept in stables—Mastiffs to guard valuable mounts, and

Cats and dogs

The main reason why cats and dogs are traditionally considered enemies is the combination of the dog's inborn chasing instinct and the cat's natural flight instinct. Few dogs can resist chasing a fleeing cat! More

---

KEY RULES FOR DOG-CAT INTRODUCTIONS

1	**Remember rewards**	Help things along by encouraging both animals to associate meeting each other with favorite treats. Rewards for being friendly work much better than punishment for misbehavior.
2	**No chasing**	Don't give the dog a chance to chase the cat. Supervise early meetings and use a crate or leash to prevent the dog from finding out that cat-chasing is fun.
3	**Beware of the claws**	A cat's claws can blind a dog. Watch out for signs that the cat is scared or angry, and also supervise play as kittens may be slow to learn claw control.

↥ *Horses and dogs can make a great team, once they learn each others' ways, but dogs unused to horses may chase them.*

ratting terriers to keep down vermin. Today, many dogs still enjoy a close relationship with horses.

See Spot ride

Most dogs are content to run behind or alongside horses, but a few more ambitious canines take up riding. Spot, a Cocker Spaniel living at a Lancashire riding school, demonstrated an unusual sense of balance when he started climbing ladders as a puppy. Soon he was riding confidently on horseback, even coping with trots and low jumps, and demonstrating his skills to raise funds for Riding for the Disabled.

Rats' guardian

In Imperial China, Pekingese dogs were bred to "live in amity with the other beasts, fish, or birds that find protection in the Imperial Palace," and Ming, a Peke belonging to Scottish naturalist

Dogs and rats are traditional enemies, but ▸▸ *Ming the Peke loved his white rats dearly.*

William Ramsay in the 1920s, certainly lived up to this ideal. With a range of friends from ravens to roe deer, his favorites were a family of white rats, which he guarded most tenderly.

Polar pals

Scientists studying the large polar bear population near Cape Churchill, Canada, were amazed to see some of the big males making friends with local Husky dogs. One bear was amazingly patient in his quest for a playmate, picking out the boldest in a line of Huskies before introducing himself with the utmost gentleness. Once the dog had accepted him, he visited every day to play with his new friend.

Bugsy of the apes

At Twycross Zoo, Leicestershire, England, Bugsy the French Bulldog was used to befriend a variety of orphan animals being brought into the house for attention, but it was a baby orangutan named Malone that aroused his paternal feelings. After one glance, he decided to adopt Malone, gently cuddling and licking him. After Malone grew too big for household life, Bugsy found a new foster-baby in Kia, a baby pygmy chimpanzee.

THE NEW AGE DOG

Alternative therapies

The "alternative" label covers a broad spectrum of treatments, some recognized and often employed by veterinarians as valuable complements or indeed alternatives to conventional methods, others distinctly dubious. All such treatments should be used only with the guidance of qualified experts, to avoid inappropriate use that may be useless or even dangerous to your pet.

Acupuncture

Acupuncture, the painless insertion of small needles at specific points of the body to stimulate self-healing, has been adopted by a growing number of veterinarians who believe it helps in the treatment of pain, chronic digestive disturbances, epilepsy, and other ailments. There is strong anecdotal evidence of its effectiveness, particularly as pain relief; indeed, dogs often fall asleep during treatment.

⬆ *Only veterinarians are licensed to treat animals with acupuncture, but a growing number of them are adopting this technique. The needles appear to cause no discomfort.*

⬆ *Homeopathic remedies may come in liquid or tablet form and are usually given orally.*

Homeopathy

Homeopathic remedies consist of "treating like with like" via intensely diluted doses of substances that would, at full strength, cause the symptoms that are to be treated, and that are said to trigger the body's immune system. There is heated debate as to whether homeopathy is valuable or useless, but many users report a good success rate. Seek advice before using homeopathic remedies, and follow instructions closely.

T-touch massage

This is a form of massage developed for treating pets by animal behaviorist Linda Tellington-Jones, in which various patterns of small circular finger movements are worked around the body. Designed to relax and reassure the patient, it is employed to resolve stress and to ease sprains, strains, and other muscle or bone disorders.

Magnet therapy

This treatment is based on treating ailments by exposure to magnetic fields. Specialized magnets worn on the body (in the case of dogs, on a collar) are said to relieve pain and speed healing. This is another technique on which the jury is still out, but many people have reported that dogs (particularly elderly arthritic animals) improved in health when provided with magnetic collars.

made at home. Always obtain expert guidance before using herbal medicines, as in some cases, overdosage can be fatal. It is best to obtain a veterinarian's diagnosis in the first place, as treating a sick dog on a trial basis is tantamount to neglect, or even cruelty.

Yoga for dogs

Canine yoga classes —or doga— originated in the United States. Dogs may not be able to achieve the lotus position, but with a little help they can work through some of the stress-busting exercises that help circulation and keep joints flexible. The combination of stretching and massage seems to be as beneficial to pets as to humans, and some owners report behavioral improvements.

▲ Herbal remedies can be very effective, but don't try making your own medicines at home unless you are fully qualified to do so.

Aromatherapy

Many dog owners recommend the use of aromatherapy oils for a range of physical ills and behavioral problems. The oil is heated in a diffuser for inhalation, or diluted (one or two drops to 5 ml of base oil) and massaged into the skin. As a general rule, stick to about 25 percent of the recommended human dosage, consult a trained aromatherapist to select appropriate oils, and seek veterinary help for problems that don't respond within a week.

▲ Stress-busting, New York style: a yoga class for the benefit of dogs and their owners.

Herbal medicine

Proprietary herbal remedies made specifically for dogs can provide safe and effective treatment, or infusions of fresh herbs can be

CANINE MISCELLANY

Beagle bed and breakfast

The world's biggest Beagle is "Sweet Willy," otherwise known as the Dog Bark Park Inn, Idaho, a unique bed and breakfast guesthouse in the form of a towering wooden dog. The 30-foot (9.2 m) model has sleeping accommodation for six, four in his belly and two in a loft room in

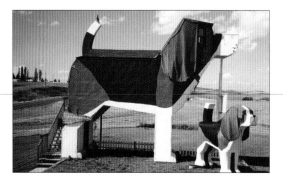

↥ *Park staff wanted Tahr captured to protect reintroduced stocks of antelope, but it took rescue workers years to win his trust.*

↥ *At the Dog Bark Park Inn, even the headboards feature carved dogs.*

his head. His creator Dennis Sullivan started with a smaller version, 12 foot (3.7 m) Toby, to help him work out the interior layout.

Waste not...

Dog mess creates an ongoing urban problem, but in San Francisco plans are afoot to turn it into an asset. As part of a recycling drive aiming to reduce the use of landfills, it is proposed to load the city's annual 6,500 tons of dog waste into a methane digester where bacteria will convert it into methane gas. This can then be used to power appliances, fuel vehicles, and generate electricity.

Canine Tarzan

In Table Mountain National Park, South Africa, a Border Collie cross nicknamed Tahr lived with the troop of baboons that raised him from puppyhood. His story began in 2001, when a bitch and her six puppies were dumped in the area. Mother and five puppies were trapped, but Tahr remained to roam the mountain. Five years later, animal welfare workers finally rescued Tahr and succesfully rehomed him in Muizenberg.

Unusual petition

Levi, a Rhodesian Ridgeback from Moray, Scotland, loved the battered sofa on which he slept, but his owner didn't, and planned to leave it behind when moving house. Her partner sided with the dog and started an on-line petition to save Levi's sofa. With more than 100 people from as far away as Germany and Finland signing up on Levi's side, his owner relented, and Levi is enjoying his old sofa in his new home.

Skydiving Dachshund

Brutus, a Miniature Dachshund, holds the record for the world's "Highest Skydiving Dog" with a 15,000-foot (4,600-m) parachute jump over California. His owner, Ron Sirull, an avid parachutist, started taking Brutus up (and down) with him because the little dog hated being left behind. However, Brutus doesn't have to operate his own para chute as he rides in his owner's jacket.

Unique graveyard

There is probably only one dog cemetery in the world that is reserved for a single breed, and it is in Alabama. At Key Underwood Coon Dog Memorial Graveyard, only Coonhounds are permitted burial, and applicants must be inspected before interment to ensure that no mongrels sneak in. Since 1937, nearly 200 Coonhounds from all over the United States have been laid to rest there.

Luxury diners

The banning of dogs from restaurants has created a new trend: restaurants designed for a canine clientele. Santa Barbara, California, boasts the world's first organic restaurant for dogs, with no salt, no sugar, and personalized "veggie bones." In Hong Kong, the six-story Dog One Life canine café offers extras from a photographic studio to a rooftop playground, as well as special catering for doggy birthday parties.

Birthday parties for dogs are now becoming popular worldwide. ▶▶

⬆ *Every Labor Day, the Tennessee Valley Coon Hunters Association gathers to celebrate their hounds at this unique dogs' graveyard.*

DOGGY DICTIONARY

Dog *(noun)* Mechanic's term for any gripping device, such as the **chain-dog**, a hooklike device under a railroad car that holds the drive chain. The etymology will be obvious to anyone who has ever tried to separate a stolen chicken bone from a dog's determined grip!

Dog *(verb)* To follow persistently, as a hound follows a scent. In the same sense we have the adjective **dogged**, meaning stubborn, determined, and persistent. Luckily, not all dogs are like this, but we have all met some whom the cap fits…

Dog cheap Something that is "dog-cheap" is very cheap indeed—a derogatory use of the term "dog."

Dog collar A slang term for a clerical collar, based on the fact that, with no opening at the front, it resembles the circular collar worn by dogs. Also, and for the same reason, a term for a ladies' broad choker necklace of the type fashionable in late Victorian and Edwardian days.

Dog days The period of greatest heat in summer, somewhere between early July and early September; named for Sirius the Dog Star, which lies in conjunction with the sun at this time and was once thought to intensify the sun's heat in the summer months.

Dog-eared Book pages that have had the corners folded down in lieu of a bookmark are said to be dog-eared, from a seeming resemblance to a hound's pendent ear. The term is now used to describe anything that is worn and shabby.

Dogfish Small members of the shark family, so called because, like dogs, they hunt in packs.

Dog-Latin Phrase or jargon imitating correct Latin.

Dogleg A sharp bend in a road, railroad line, or golf fairway, named from the pronounced bend in a dogs' hind leg. In medieval castles, passages leading to the garderobes generally had a dog-leg approach to prevent the foul air from the privy pit blowing directly back into the room!

Dog rose The wild rose is said to derive this name from the traditional use of the root to cure the bite of a mad dog.

Dog star Sirius, the brightest star in the night sky. It is located in the constellation of Canis Major ("big dog"), said to represent one of the hounds of the hunter Orion, hence its nickname.

Dogwatch At sea, the dogwatch is the work shift between 16.00 and 20.00. It may be a corruption of "dodge watch." This shift is split into two two-hour periods (first and second dogwatches) so that, by rotation, the men avoid ("dodge") standing the same watches every day. For lovers of puns, novelist Patrick O'Brien came up with a splendid explanation: the shortened watch is called a dogwatch "because it is cur-tailed."

Dogwood Nobody quite knows how this attractive tree got its name. It may come from the fact that a concoction of the leaves was used to treat mange in dogs. Or it may be a corruption of "dag-wood," its hard wood being used to make "dags," wooden skewers used to cook meat over an open fire.

Hot dog A frankfurter sausage served hot in a bun. The name probably arose as an American joke related to 19th-century German immigrants, who introduced both frankfurter sausages and Dachshund "sausage dogs" to the United States. The first recorded use of the term is from 1895, but jokes about the suspicious contents of sausages go back a lot further.

CANINE COMMENTS

Unfair to dogs

The dog may be known as Man's Best Friend, but many of our everyday figures of speech treat canines as the yardstick of undesirability. Young men describe an unattractive girl as "a dog," and the same term is used by professionals ranging from jewelers to real estate agents to indicate worthless goods. This derogatory usage is common to many languages and cultures, regardless of actual canine status.

A dog's life

To **"lead a dog's life"** is to have a wretched existence, harking back to the days when dogs were kept in poor conditions, scavenging for scraps. Similarly, we speak of personal or financial ruin as **"going to the dogs,"** or dying in miserable circumstances as **"to die like a dog."** From the same linguistic kennel comes the expression, **"Every dog has its day,"** or even the lowest of the low has his moment.

Canine observation

Many popular "doggy" sayings are simply based on observation. From the image of a dog collapsing into sleep after a good walk we have the phrase **"dog-tired,"** from a dog's joyful tail-wag the simile, **"Happy as a dog with two tails,"** and from the woeful expression of a dog anticipating a rebuke the description **"hangdog."** Most dog owners will also appreciate the accuracy of the simile **"sick as a dog,"** too.

Let sleeping dogs lie

This common saying is good dog management as well as a handy way of warning people not to stir up trouble in a situation that is currently peaceful.

Dog eat dog

The expression "It's a dog-eat-dog world," meaning a world of ruthless competition, dates back to the 1930s and is commonly used today. It's actually a reversal of a much older proverb, "Dog does not eat dog," or people of the same kind, or with the same interests, do not destroy each other, a reversal that may be seen as a sad commentary on modern society.

Putting on the dog

The expression "to put on dog" (without a "the") was American college slang in the late 19th century, when it meant "to put on airs." Some people link the expression with fashionable ladies "wearing" expensive lapdogs as part of their outfits; but it was probably a development from the term "doggy," which meant "fancy" or "stylish" at the time. Today, "putting on the dog" generally means "dressing up flashily."

Doggy proverbs

Don't keep a dog and bark yourself. (English)
The dog's kennel is not the place to keep a sausage. (Danish)
Beware of a silent dog and still water. (Latin)
Three things best avoided: a strange dog, a flood, and a man who thinks himself wise. (Welsh)
Those who sleep with dogs will rise with fleas. (Italian)
The greatest love is a mother's; then a dog's; then a sweetheart's. (Polish)
A good dog deserves a good bone. (American)
Don't respond to a barking dog. (Moroccan)
One dog barks at something; the rest bark at him. (Chinese)
A house without a cat or a dog is the house of a scoundrel. (Portuguese)

INDEX

Page numbers set in *italics* refer to picture captions.

DOG BIZ

DOG BIZ

Photographic Credits

The Art Archive: 14 left (Musée du Louvre, Paris/Dagli Orti), 42 left (Bibliothèque Nationale Paris/Harper Collins Publishers), 56 left (Harper Collins Publishers), 58 bottom left (Private Collection), 70 top left (British Museum/Dagli Orti [A]), 75 top center (Culver Pictures), 104 bottom right (National Anthropological Museum, Mexico/Dagli Orti), 106 bottom left (Galleria Borghese, Rome/Dagli Orti [A]), 108 bottom right (Dagli Orti), 109 center right (Museo del Prado, Madrid/Dagli Orti [A]), 110 left (Tate Gallery, London/Eileen Tweedy), 110 bottom right (Nicolas Sapieha), 118 bottom left, 119 top left (Dagli Orti [A]), 130 top (Musée du Louvre, Paris/Dagli Orti), 130 bottom (Tate Gallery, London/Eileen Tweedy), 133 top left (Marc Charmet), 154 left (Private Collection/Marc Charmet), 158 both/159 right/161 bottom (Poggio Petroio Dog Collection/Nicolas Sapieha).
The Bridgeman Art Library: 36 (Josef Mensing Gallery, Germany), 41 bottom (Roy Miles Fine Paintings), 44 top (Private Collection), 50 top (Private Collection), 60 bottom left (Private Collection), 81 top right (Private Collection), 111 bottom right (© Nationalmuseum, Stockholm), 131 top (© Yale Center for British Art, Paul Mellon Collection, USA), 131 bottom (Private Collection), 140 left (Ham House, Surrey/The Stapleton Collection), 193 top (Private Collection/© Partridge Fine Arts, London).
British Manchester Terrier Club: 46 center right.
Jane Burton, Warren Photographic: 1 (dog), 2, 4 top, 11, 22-3, 25 top, 30 center left, 32 top left, 32 bottom left, 32-3, 35 top, 69, 101, 126 center right, 136-7, 139 right, 151 top, 171 (dog), 178 bottom, 192.
Carriage Dog Society: 97 right (Marion Creed).
The Cheetah Conservation Fund: 53 bottom right (Patricia Tricorache).
Coondogcemetery.com: 197 bottom left (Drew Werndli).
Aidan Crawley: 91 top.
Dog Bark Park Inn: 196 top left and center.
Emma Animal Rescue Society, Tears: 196 top right.
Fortean Picture Library: 112 left (Janet and Colin Bord), 113 bottom (Anthony Wallis), 117 right.
Illustrated London News Picture Library: 141 top left.
Inn Sign Society: 190 bottom right, 191 bottom right.
Interpet Archive: 24 lower left, 25 lower right, 31 top right, 38 right, 81 top center, 115 top, 148 all, 199 top right, 152 top left, 153 top right, 157 bottom, 171 all, 172 top, 178 top right, 179 both, 180 left, 184 both.
iStockphoto.com/
Aldra: 62 left.
Ira Bachinskaya: 5, 18 center left, 57 top.
Danny Bailey: 54 left.
Galina Barskaya: 147 center left.
Tamara Bauer: 39 top.
Nicholas Belton: 17 top.
Arnstein Berg: 65 bottom.
Debi Bishop: 52 top.
Dan Brandenburg: 30 top right.
Alexander Briel: 155 (cartoon dog).

Henri Caroline: 153 top.
Roberta Casaliggi: 16 center left.
Caziopeia: 157 top.
Gregg Cerenzio: 138 top.
Ranjan Chari: 64 left.
Michael Chen: 109 top right.
Peter Chen: 174-6 (zodiac symbols).
Kit Sen Chin: 19 top, 21 top center, 28 bottom right, 143 center right top, 143 center right bottom.
Kelly Cline: 195 right.
Odelia Cohen: 152 bottom.
Christiane Cornelius: 1 (zodiac), 175 (zodiac).
Ctulu: 180 right.
Jodie Davies: 24 top.
Julie de Leseleuc: 177 (symbols).
Diane Diederich: 21 top left, 113 top, 155 left (cake).
Duckycards: 4 bottom.
DWphotos: 186.
Eyecrave: 156.
Marianne Fitzgerald: 177 top.
Angus Forbes: 97 top.
Cristina Fumi: 194 top.
Mark G.: 84 bottom.
Mugur Geana: 88.
Robin George: 73 top.
Amy Goodchild: 112 bottom right.
Walter Green: 134 left.
Bill Gruber: 98 top.
Peter Guess: 147 bottom right.
Jostein Hauge: 189 bottom.
Angela Hill: 29 bottom right.
Justin Horrocks: 60 top, 115 bottom.
Dawn Hudson: 144 top.
Izold: 17 bottom right, 21 top right.
Tracie Jibbens: 37.
P.J. Jones: 143 center left bottom.
Cheryl Kardas: 17 bottom left center.
Antti Karppinen: 6, 23 top right, 149 center left.
Sergey Kashkin: 154 bottom.
Tan Kian Koon: 105 top.
Serguei Kovalev: 188 top left.
Bernd Klumpp: 51 bottom.
Laurie Knight: 26 bottom left.
Lyle Koehnlein: 114 left.
Robin Krauss: 105 bottom.
Arthur Kwiatkowski: 176.
Erik Lam: 56 top, 150 bottom.
JinYoung Lee: 98 bottom left.
Kate Leigh: 182 left.
Karen Libby: 44 bottom.
Jason Lugo: 188 bottom left.
Mika Makkonen: 160 top.
Jurie Maree: 67 bottom.
Markanja: 21 bottom right, 22 center left.